Creative
Jewish
Education

Creative
Jewish
Education

■ ■ ■ A Reconstructionist Perspective

Edited by
Jeffrey L. Schein and Jacob J. Staub

Reconstructionist Rabbinical College Press

 and

Rossel Books ■ ■ ■ Chappaqua, New York

Library of Congress Cataloging in Publication Data
Main entry under title:

Creative Jewish education.

Bibliography: p.
1. Jewish religious education—United States—Addresses, essays, lectures.   2.   Reconstructionist   Judaism—Addresses,   essays, lectures.   I. Schein, Jeffrey L.   II. Staub, Jacob J.
BM103.C74   1985   296.6'8   85-14260
ISBN 0-940646-33-1 (pbk.)

© *Copyright 1985 by Reconstructionist Rabbinical College*

Published by **Reconstructionist Rabbinical College Press** *and* **Rossel Books**, 44 Dunbow Drive, Chappaqua, NY 10514, (914) 238-8954.

First Edition

Cover design by Shai Zauderer.
Composition by Diana Levine Computer Typesetting.
Manufactured in the United States of America.

For

Annette Temin

Members of the Bernstein, Harris, Schein, and Seidman families have contributed generously to the publication of this volume in loving memory of:

■ ■ ■ Acknowledgments

First and foremost, we want to express our profound appreciation to Annette Temin, to whom this volume is dedicated. It is because of her unending encouragement and support that we were first motivated to begin this project and were then able to proceed to its completion. Even beyond our appreciation for her support for this specific volume, we acknowledge her lifelong career as a Jewish educator and as a supporter both of Jewish education and of Reconstructionism.

The contributions of members of the Bernstein, Harris, Schein, and Seidman families in memory of loved ones also deserve special recognition, because they epitomize the spirit that, we hope, permeates this volume. Jewish education is, after all, an enterprise which seeks to sustain the chain of the generations. That this particular enterprise has been sustained in part by *tzedakah* in memory of our loved ones, may their memories be for a blessing, is a sign that our efforts to present our tradition in innovative ways are part of the continuing evolution of the Jewish tradition.

In line with this, we consider this volume an offering to our wives, Debbie and Barbara, and to our children, Benjamin Haviv, Leah Esther, Jonah Hanan, Andrew Hillel, and Hana Sivya. It is they who have had to be understanding – as they have done so well – as the demands of our work conflict with the legitimate needs of our families. We are very grateful to them.

We thank the contributors to this volume whose patience has been tried through many lengthy delays as we have proceeded slowly to publication.

The essays in this volume are indebted primarily to the work of Rabbi Mordecai M. Kaplan, z'l, whose program for the reconstruction of Jewish civilization has been the moving force and the source of creativity for the reconstruction of Jewish education; Rabbi Ira Eisenstein, whose leadership has established and sustained the Reconstructionist institutions in which we and most of the contributors have been nourished; and Reconstructionist thinkers such as Jack J. Cohen and Meir Ben-Horin, who have contributed to this collection and whose writings on Jewish education have had a formative influence on the approach of contemporary Reconstructionist educators.

We are also indebted to Society Hill Synagogue's Ann Spak Thal School, which has served for many years as a laboratory school for students of the Reconstructionist Rabbinical College. Both editors of this volume received tremendous stimulation from years served on the staff of the school. The pragmatic orientation of the Reconstructionist approach demands that theory and practice be closely linked. The Thal School has served as such a link for many others as well.

Special thanks are due to Susan H. Haubenstock, for her careful copy editing of the entire manuscript.

Finally, we are grateful for the existence of the Reconstructionist Rabbinical College. Not only have we both been trained at the RRC, but the warm, nurturing, and truly communal atmosphere of the College gave birth to our relationship with each other, a friendship that has extended far beyond collegiality and that has deepened as we have worked together on this project.

Jeffrey L. Schein
Jacob J. Staub
Wyncote, Pennsylvania
March 1, 1984
27 Adar I 5744

■ ■ ■ Contents

Pointing Towards the Future

■ ■ ■ Contributors

Joel Alpert (RRC '76) currently serves as Director of Religious Education of Congregation Keneseth Israel in Elkins Park, Pennsylvania, and is an adjunct member of the faculty of the Reconstructionist Rabbinical College. He first developed the Shabbat Seder program with Rebecca T. Alpert at Society Hill Synagogue's Ann Spak Thal School.

Meir Ben-Horin is Professor Emeritus of Education at the Dropsie College for Hebrew and Cognate Learning, and an editor of *Jewish Social Studies*.

David Blumenthal is the Jay and Leslie Cohen Professor of Judaic Studies at Emory University. He is also Director of the Fred R. Crawford Witness to the Holocaust Project and a Special Advisor to the Chairman of the Holocaust Memorial Council.

David Brusin (RRC '74) serves as the Headmaster of the Hillel Day School of Tampa, Florida. He formerly served as Director of Education at Niles Township Jewish Congregation in Skokie, Illinois, where the program described was first developed.

Sara Caine is currently the fifth- and sixth-grade Jewish Studies teacher at Solomon Schechter Day School in Bala Cynwyd, Pennsylvania. She is a Ph.D. candidate in Second Language Acquisition at the University of Pennsylvania.

Jack J. Cohen has served as the Director of the B'nai B'rith Hillel Foundations in Israel since 1961. He served as Educational Director of Park Synagogue in Cleveland (1943-45), Director of the Jewish Reconstructionist Foundation (1945-54), and Rabbi of the Society for the Advancement of Judaism (1954-61). He is the author of *The Case for Religious Naturalism* and *Jewish Education in a Democratic Society*, and has published widely in leading periodicals in the United States and Israel.

Nancy Fuchs-Kreimer (RRC '82) serves as Director of the Mordecai M. Kaplan Institute for Adult Jewish Studies of the Reconstructionist Rabbinical College.

Paula Halfon is currently the sixth-grade General Studies teacher at Solomon Schechter Day School in Bala Cynwyd, Pennsylvania. In addition to her experience in elementary education, she has had extensive experience in Jewish camping and afternoon Hebrew School settings.

Beth Kellman serves as Judaic Studies Consultant for the Bureau of Jewish Education of San Francisco, Marin County, and the Peninsula. She created the family programs described here as Director of Education at Congregation Rodef Sholom in San Rafael, California.

Harold Kushner is Rabbi of Temple Israel in Natick, Massachusetts, and author of *When Children Ask About God* (Reconstructionist Press, 1971) and *When Bad Things Happen To Good People* (Schocken, 1981). He has also helped to edit two prayer books, *Likrat Shabbat* and *Mahzor Hadash*.

Etan Levine serves on the faculty of the University of Haifa.

Norman A. Newberg is Associate Professor in the Educational Leadership Progam of the Graduate School of Education at the University of Pennsylvania. He has taught courses in "Modern Midrash" and "Psychological Aspects of the Jewish Life Cycle" at the Reconstructionist Rabbinical College. His current research concerns instructional leadership.

Jeffrey L. Schein (RRC '77) serves as Educational Director at Congregation Or Ami in Lafayette Hills, Pennsylvania, and as Director of Jewish Education at the Reconstructionist Rabbinical College.

Peninnah Schram is Assistant Professor of Speech and Drama at Stern College of Yeshiva University and a professional storyteller. Her two record albums, *A Storyteller's Journey I* and *II*, have received recommendations from reviewers, including the Children's Services Division of the New York Public Library. She performs stories and conducts workshops across the country on the art of storytelling.

Sidney H. Schwarz (RRC '80) is currently the Executive Director of the Jewish Community Council of Greater Washington, D.C. He served for eight years as Rabbi of Reconstructionist Congregation Beth Israel in Media, Pennsylvania. He has served on the faculties of the Reconstructionist Rabbinical College, Akiba Hebrew Academy, and Gratz College, and is the founding editor of *Raayonot*, the journal of the Reconstructionist Rabbinical Association.

Jacob J. Staub (RRC '77) is the Director of the Department of Medieval Civilization at the Reconstructionist Rabbinical College and editor of *Reconstructionist*. His article here is based upon his experiences teaching undergraduates at Lafayette College and Washington University.

Steven Stroiman (RRC '74) teaches at Akiba Hebrew Academy in Philadelphia. He has been a member of the Unstructured Synagogue havurah since 1970. His doctoral dissertation was a study of the group development of a havurah.

Cynthia Toback is currently the Learning Center Director of Niles Township Jewish Congregation in Skokie, Illinois. She also serves on the Professional Growth Committee of the Chicago Board of Jewish Education.

The Application of Reconstructionist Concepts to Jewish Education

■ ■ ■ **Jeffrey L. Schein and Jacob J. Staub**

Over the last fifteen years, Jewish education in America has undergone a renaissance. The quality of educational materials now available, the varieties of innovative methodologies that have been developed to transmit these new materials, the examples of creative programming aimed at meeting the changing needs of Jewish life: all of these make our collective resources great. Nevertheless, the development of these resources has not been matched by the development of adequate vehicles for sharing them. The initial impetus for the publication of this volume arose out of a desire to address this problem. In collecting some of the best educational resources of the Reconstructionist movement, we hope to make them more available to Jewish educators of all orientations who share a concern about the quality of Jewish education. It is our hope and expectation that readers of this volume will find the analyses and descriptions of educational programs collected here to be suggestive and illuminating.

We hope that the non-Reconstructionist reader will be comfortable utilizing these resources. We are confident that the elements of "good education" in the essays below will speak for themselves. Creative teaching, a love of Jewish tradition, and a keen sense of classroom realities are not the exclusive property of any single movement in Jewish life. To the extent that those elements are present here, they should be shared liberally with all concerned Jewish educators. If, as we believe is the case, Reconstructionist thinking adds coherence and vigor to good Jewish education, the non-Reconstructionist reader will also find in this volume many opportunities to understand the Reconstructionist approach to Jewish life.

This, of course, brings us to the task of distinguishing a Reconstructionist approach to Jewish education from other approaches. Comparisons with the educational ventures of other movements are often invidious or self-serving. Rather, we have chosen to develop the Reconstructionist approach internally, by turning to four central concepts of Reconstructionist thinking: The Americanization of Jewish Education; Living in Two Civilizations; Judaism as an Evolving Religious Civilization; and Commitment to Intellectual Integrity.

We have proceeded as follows. First, we delineate the four classical Reconstructionist concepts that bear directly upon education, according to which the contributions to this volume are arranged. In each case, the concept is explained briefly in classical Reconstructionist terms; the ways in which the contributions reflect the concept are articulated; and observations are offered about new considerations arising in the contributions that modify the classical concept. In this way, we attempt to illustrate how contemporary practice has begun to reconstruct the theory, and to highlight the fact that a new generation of Jewish children shares many, but not all, of the needs of previous generations.

Having completed each of these sections, the thoughtful reader undoubtedly will be left with several questions. We recognize that many of the classical Reconstructionist concerns were organically related, so that the categories in which various articles appear may seem puzzling and arbitrary. For example, part of the process of enabling American Jews to live comfortably and creatively in two civilizations involved the definition of Judaism as an evolving Jewish civilization. Thus, each of the essays inevitably reflects more than one of the classical concerns.

More fundamentally, we anticipate that the inquiring reader may ask two questions: first, what is the role of the concept of peoplehood—generally recognized as the most significant Reconstructionist contribution to the self-definition of American Jewry—in a Reconstructionist approach to Jewish education? And second, beyond the specific programmatic suggestions contained in each essay, what form would a broad outline of a Reconstructionist curriculum take?

In our minds, these two questions are inseparable. The Reconstructionist curriculum of the future must be based on a careful consideration of the role of peoplehood in the Judaism of the present and future, as well as the past. The editors' essay, "Towards a Spiritualization of Peoplehood," attempts to provide such an analysis, as well as to provide a point of departure for future efforts to develop Reconstructionist curricula. Jack J. Cohen's essay, "The Ideal Jew," provides an important counterpart to the editors' essay by articulating the goals of Jewish education that remain part of the unfinished agenda of Jewish educators of every conceivable orientation. Together, the two essays point to two areas to which Jewish educators need to apply themselves in the future.

The Americanization of Jewish Education

From the beginning, one of the central tenets of the Reconstructionist orientation to Jewish education has been the Americanization of the techniques utilized to transmit Judaism to children. The methods of the Eastern European *heder* were judged authoritarian and archaic, capable neither of teaching nor of inspiring new generations of American Jewish children. Thus, Reconstructionist educators sought to make Jewish education "progressive"—where the term bore the connotations of "forward-looking" and "democratic," and accorded with the general philosophy of education expounded by John Dewey.

While few Jewish educators today would advocate a return to the *heder*, many reject the notion, once widely held, that Jewish schools should be modeled on the American public school system. Public education does not command the esteem it was granted a half century ago. Innovative techniques and curricula have come and gone, and even in the infrequent cases where they have endured successfully, Jewish educators often find that they are not applicable to the unique needs and goals of the Jewish school. Values clarification and moral education, for example, have been criticized as inappropriate vehicles for the transmission of the Jewish heritage.

In reaction to the enthusiastic embrace in the past by Jewish educators of secular educational methods, there is currently a tendency abroad among Jewish educators to reject such models out of hand and to cultivate uniquely Jewish models of curriculum and instruction. While contemporary Reconstructionists may not share fully the enthusiasm of their predecessors about American educational methods, the legacy of the movement's founders remains apparent: the Reconstructionist educator is always aware of the potential contribution of the American civilization (of which educational theory and practice is a prominent part) to the Jewish needs of the individual. Thus, the Reconstructionist approach to contemporary Jewish education can be of service here by emphasizing the obvious: the possibility of a creative synthesis—one that attempts to evaluate the utility and appropriateness of secular models for the needs of the Jewish school while avoiding the pitfalls of uncritical imitation.

Two of the contributions address this question and adopt this approach. "Incorporating Secular Models of Learning into the Jewish School," originally composed as a curriculum by a group of rabbinical students at the Reconstructionist Rabbinical College and revised for this volume by Jeffrey L. Schein, reflects an effort to incorporate creatively the best models of public education into a non-graded, open classroom Jewish synagogue school. "A Breath of Fresh Learning," by David Brusin and Cynthia Toback, describes an adaptation of Teacher Learning Centers—initiated in pubic schooling—to the curricular needs of the Jewish afternoon school.

Living in Two Civilizations

Integrally related to the goal of the Americanization of Jewish education has been the Reconstructionist ideal of living in two civilizations—a Jewish civilization that links Jews to other Jews around the world, and an American civilization which links them to non-Jewish Americans. One direct consequence of this analysis was Kaplan's insistence that American Jews should enroll their children in public schools. It was the assumed function of public schools to initiate all American children into the rich political, intellectual, and cultural legacy of American civilization. Inasmuch as American Jews, according to Kaplan, live primarily in the American and secondarily in the Jewish civilization, such an initiation was indispensable. Effective supplementary Jewish education, working in concert with the synagogue and the Jewish home, could, he believed, provide an adequate foundation for a child's participation in Jewish civilization.

Much has happened over the last five decades to call into question this fundamental postulate of classical Reconstructionist educational thought. The Federation of Reconstructionist Congregations and Havurot itself has, in this last decade, called for the establishment of more Jewish day schools. In her article, "Teaching About Other Religions," Nancy Fuchs-Kreimer wrestles with both the philosophical and the practical dimensions of the dilemma: How can we offer an intensive Jewish education without abandoning our commitment to living in two civilizations? Her proposed "fantasy" of a multi-cultural day school center is, in theory, a way to reconstruct the Kaplanian ideal in light of the altered circumstances which confront American Jews in the 1980s. The current conventional wisdom, widely accepted by Jewish educators, declares that Jewish day schools are the only effective means at our disposal to acculturate children into the Jewish civilization. It is thus significant that the classical legacy to which Reconstructionist educators are heir keeps alive the issue of the balance between our Jewish and our American commitments.

In the best of all possible Reconstructionist worlds, our Jewish and American commitments are integrated as well as balanced. One of the most exciting developments within the curricula of Jewish day schools has been the attempt to integrate Jewish and secular studies. The article "Integrating Jewish and Secular Studies in the Jewish Day School," by

Sara Caine and Paula Halfon, provides an educational framework for fusing two strands of the day school curriculum. If such attempts succeed in removing the hyphen from the identity of American-Jewish children, there may yet be another reason for Reconstructionist support of day schools.

As Fuchs-Kreimer suggests in her essay, preceding generations seem to have overestimated the efficacy of formal, supplementary Jewish schooling. With regard to public education, Christopher Lasch (in his book *Inequality*) and others have questioned the assumption that we can rely primarily on formal schooling to socialize our children in desired ways. Rather, they argue that it is the informal social mechanisms – the family, the peer group, the media – that educate most profoundly.

Such insights confirm the classical Reconstructionist analysis of civilizational identity. What has changed, however, since Kaplan first described the indispensable function to be played by the Jewish family and community in the process of Jewish acculturation, is the ability of contemporary American Jewish families to execute this role. As we progress further from the natural, deep ethnicity of the immigrant generation, we can no longer assume that Jewish parents have a knowledge of and a comfort with Jewish sancta that would enable them to socialize their children unassisted. Accordingly, Jewish educators have become increasingly sensitive to the urgent need of educating the family as a unit.

In "Family Days and Family Education," Beth Kellman explores the programmatic possibilities that emerge from the attempt to address this new circumstance. She offers a framework for promoting a new relationship between Jewish parents and the Jewish school, in which parents can become active partners in the Jewish education of their children. Detailed examples of Family Days in the synagogue school, adaptable to other Jewish settings, are offered.

The articles by Rabbi Kaplan and by Joel Alpert about the Shabbat Seder update an original suggestion first made by Kaplan in *Judaism as a Civilization* (1934). A decade ago, Kaplan renewed his call, in the *Reconstructionist* article reprinted here, for an adaptation of the Pesah Seder to be instituted on Shabbat Eve, as a means of promoting Jewish learning in the natural setting of the home. This proposal has since been developed and elaborated in the broader Jewish community. Alpert's article illustrates how contemporary Reconstructionist educators have incorporated the idea in the programs of Jewish schools and synagogues, in order to provide complete family units with a taste of the Shabbat experience and a model for enriching their weekly Shabbat celebrations.

Finally, in "A Practical Guide in the Formation of a Havurah," Steven Stroiman discusses yet another way to counteract the fragmentation that occurs when Jewish learning is relegated to the formal classroom. The

Reconstructionist Press first published the pamphlet "The Havurah Idea," by Jacob Neusner and Ira Eisenstein, two decades ago—a pamphlet describing the exciting possibilities which the havurah offered as a means of Jewish study and celebration. The time was not then ripe for the idea to take root in the Jewish community. Today, however, havurot flourish both within and independent of synagogues, and have achieved a popularity that derives, at least in part, from the dissolution of the extended family and the impersonal nature of large synagogues. It is tempting to argue that the havurah is the most Reconstructionist of all the programmatic suggestions offered in this volume—in its re-creation of the organic community in miniature, in the self-reliance of its members as they struggle directly to come to terms with the tradition, and in its democratic structure. A large percentage of Reconstructionist synagogues have begun as havurot; all of them seek to retain the best features of the havurah, and many continue to retain the havurah's structure and label. The preliminary connections that have been established over the last several years between The National Havurah Committee and the Federations of Reconstructionist Congregations and Havurot are yet another confirmation of this point. It is not by chance that the Havurah movement has found Reconstructionist offices most hospitable. Stroiman draws upon his broad experience in initiating havurot to offer guidelines for forming and maintaining such groups.

In the Reconstructionist formulation of living in two civilizations, creative Jewish life in the Diaspora is linked to a vital interconnection with the State of Israel. Both the cognitive and affective dimensions of *Ahavat Zion* (the love of Israel) are thus of crucial importance to Jewish education. The article "Six Theses," by Meir Ben-Horin, focuses both upon the way in which the State of Israel has transformed our view of the world, as well as the challenges which that new worldview poses to Jewish education. As a cultural/spiritual Zionist, Ben-Horin suggests that the Jewish educator ought to do more than secure the loyalty of American Jewish children to the State of Israel; he challenges us to recognize and respond to the transformations wrought upon our self-understanding by the existence of Israel.

The "Simulation of the Sixth Zionist Congress," developed by the staff of Society Hill Synagogue's Ann Spak Thal School, was designed to help elementary and junior high students experience the emotional depth of the age-old Jewish commitment to the land of Israel as the Jewish homeland, a commitment which perhaps—on logical and pragmatic grounds— should have been superseded by an acceptance of the Uganda option.

Judaism as an Evolving Religious Civilization

The Reconstructionist orientation to Jewish life answers the perennial quest for a definition of Judaism by defining Judaism as an evolving religious civilization of the Jewish people. Etan Levine's article, "Educational Implications of Reconstructionism," which is reprinted here from the *Reconstructionist*, outlines in a broad way the consequences of such a view of Jewish life for the curriculum and pedagogy of the Jewish school.

Because Judaism is a civilization as well as a religion, Reconstructionists seek to incorporate the folk resources of the Jewish people into the curriculum of the Jewish school. Folk tales are one of these resources. In "Ethical and Folk Components of Jewish Storytelling," Peninnah Schram discusses the ways that the folk culture of the Jewish people can be used to reinforce the ethical and the monotheistic themes of Jewish life. Exploration of the effects of imaginal folk themes on the moral development of children is at the heart of Bruno Bettelheim's work *The Uses of Enchantment*. Schram reminds us that Jewish storytellers have been utilizing some of these same resources for millenia, and she proposes ways in which this crucial component of Jewish acculturation can be introduced again into our curricula.

Similarly, Norman A. Newberg's "Nurturing Biblical Fantasies," which is discussed more fully in the following section of this essay, is another instance of the attempt to help Jewish students identify with and thus internalize the narratives of the tradition and their protagonists.

The evolving nature of Jewish civilization that Reconstructionists affirm also has significant consequences in the classroom. The Reconstructionist educator bears a responsibility to shape the curriculum in ways that manifest and transmit the corollaries of the evolutionary view: that the beliefs and customs of Jewish civilization have not remained unchanged since Sinai, but have rather developed over the centuries as the Jewish people have adapted to new circumstances and have incorporated the best of the non-Jewish civilizations with which they have come into contact; that the unity of the Jewish people over the course of their history has been maintained by including a diversity of interpretations of beliefs and customs, so that there is usually no simple way to explain what Jews believe about any issue; and that, as a consequence, each individual bears the responsibility for what he understands or does not understand, for which practices she observes or does not observe.

While this view of Judaism cannot be taught in a direct theoretical way to young students, the shape of the curricula to which they are exposed year after year can and should reflect this philosophy, so that, as they mature, they can emerge from their Jewish education with the orientation and the knowledge required to approach the tradition from this evolutionary perspective. Educators need to avoid, on the one hand, curricular models that have the effect of indoctrinating the student about what Judaism is and what is correct from the Jewish standpoint. Thus, overly personal or charismatic interpretations of Jewish life, however effective they are in motivating students, must give way to curricula that include a diversity of perspectives taken from the riches of the tradition. On the other hand, attempts to reduce the scope of the Jewish curriculum for the sake of pedagogical effectiveness are also to be avoided. It is not acceptable to the Reconstructionist educator for students to learn the Hebrew language, or the Torah, or the history of modern Zionism, or any other single facet of the Jewish experience, at the expense of a broader exposure to the variety of Jewish expressions over the ages.

A concern with the presentation of a full and accurate portrait of Judaism is at the heart of the two articles, "Doing Justice to *Tzedakah*" and "Faith in God After the Holocaust: An Educational Encounter," by Jeffrey L. Schein. The program described in the first article is based on the thesis that, while contemporary approaches to teaching *tzedakah* may be creative, they are all based on fragmentary representations of the Jewish understanding of *tzedakah*. The second article describes a program in which groups of teens or adults can encounter four Jewish thinkers, and is based upon the premise that an introduction to Jewish theology and its response to tragedy is most effective when it helps individuals to grapple with a variety of theological responses from different stages in Jewish history.

Commitment to Intellectual Integrity

A basic premise of the Reconstructionist approach to Judaism is that one's intellectual integrity need not and ought not be compromised in the affirmation of one's Jewish identity. There is, to be sure, a perpetual tension that must be maintained between traditional formulations of Jewish belief and the contemporary views that a Jew today finds compelling, so that the tradition is given a credible voice in influencing and modifying the contemporary understanding of reality. Under no circumstances, however, would the Reconstructionist position advocate that a contemporary Jew abandon her view of the truth to accept dishonestly a traditional view of which she is not convinced. It is this consideration that led to Kaplan's transnaturalistic conception of God and on which the Reconstructionist versions of the traditional liturgy have been based.

It is for this reason that Kaplanian and other Reconstructionist interpretations of the concept of God and of other pillars of Jewish belief are not binding, in a dogmatic way, upon Jews who call themselves Reconstructionists. Kaplan's approach to God, for example, is inseparable from and actually rests upon a prior commitment to intellectual integrity.

Kaplan himself had a great deal of tolerance for Jews who genuinely held beliefs at odds with his own. He had little tolerance, however, for those who did not share his commitment to intellectual integrity. He rejected, on both Jewish and philosophical grounds, the notion that intellectual questioning could and should be suspended so that religion might provide a message of salvation and comfort.

Thus, the task of the Reconstructionist educator is not to indoctrinate students in a Reconstructionist orthodoxy, but rather to aid them in their own intellectual quests. Sidney Schwarz's "Reconstructing Teachers and Curricula," reprinted from *Reconstructionist*, elaborates the important ways in which such intellectual integrity should be manifested by the faculty and in the specific curricular areas of the Jewish afternoon school. David Blumenthal's "On Teaching the Holocaust," reprinted from *Reconstructionist*, and Jacob Staub's "Teaching Jewish Studies to Undergraduates" discuss similar concerns with regard to the academic context. Both articles echo the often-heard criticism that Jewish education is juvenile in scope, content, and tone. Adult Jewish education and Jewish Studies at the college and university level are as deserving of the creative and experimental energies of Jewish educators as are synagogue and day school programs.

Harold Kushner's "The Idea of God in the Jewish Classroom" is representative of the continuing attempts of Reconstructionists to come to terms with the concept of God. Though Reconstructionism is often identified exclusively with Kaplan's transnaturalistic descriptions of God, there have been, in the spirit of ongoing reconstruction, revisions and internal critiques of Kaplan's theology by subsequent Reconstructionist thinkers. Among the most notable are Harold Schulweis' work on Predicate Theology, and the continuing efforts of Kushner, the author of the recent best seller, *When Bad Things Happen to Good People*, to amplify the human dimensions of religious naturalism. Kushner's first book, *When Children Ask About God*, was published by the Reconstructionist Press. In his essay in this volume, he provides a description of some of the exercises he employs in the classroom when he is called upon to teach children about God.

Finally, it is significant that Kaplan's definition of intellectual integrity is itself subject to revision. Kaplan's understanding of truth was conditioned by the social and cultural milieu from which he emerged. From a contemporary perspective, his assumptions that the truth is attainable rationally, and that its attainment has socially melioristic consequences, seem dated. In an age of bi-hemispheric neurological research, our understanding of human learning and perception is being revolutionized. Norman Newberg's "Nurturing Biblical Fantasies" emphasizes the role of emotions in Jewish learning, and specifically the role which emotional empathy plays in leading to a more sophisticated understanding of narratives such as the *Akedah*. The essay is suggestive of future directions that Reconstructionist thought may take as we confront the arational causes of our consonance and dissonance with the tradition. Such lines of inquiry may be able to assist us in understanding why traditional modes of thought that apparently conflict with our avowed beliefs nevertheless resonate in our spiritual quests in ways that are difficult to explain.

Incorporating Secular Models of Learning into the Jewish School

■ ■ ■ Jeffrey L. Schein

The Ann Spak Thal School at Society Hill Synagogue in Philadelphia was begun as an experimental "open classroom" afternoon Hebrew school in the fall of 1973. Three years later a curriculum was written for the school. This inverted the normal relationship between a curriculum and the teaching/learning process. Normally a curriculum is thought to guide (or even determine) the educational experiences of children.

Yet, if a curriculum is to guide intelligently it must be based on the real life experiences of teachers and students. The Reconstructionist Rabbinical College students who initiated the Ann Spak Thal School believed, as they began their project in 1973, that a curricular moratorium was necessary. If new ways to teach old traditions were to be found, the staff would need the freedom to experiment, fail, and learn. The question of which techniques from secular education were appropriate for Jewish education could not be answered *a priori*. Learning models from secular education took on concrete meaning as the staff of the Ann Spak Thal School struggled to create a different kind of afternoon Hebrew school environment. They also became appropriately "Judaized" as the interaction between Jewish content, educational goals, and the needs of the learner developed. Occasionally, techniques were abandoned because they seemed "un-Jewish." More often, the techniques were modified to fit the needs of a Jewish school.

What follows are selected aspects of the curriculum that was written in 1976, three years after the founding of the school. Each aspect—

institutionalizing of creativity, non-aged group instruction, Jewish social studies, and a model of the learning process—represents an attempt to integrate models drawn from secular education with the non-secular Jewish goals of the school. Each aspect is described in the language of the 1976 curriculum. Readers should know, however, that the Ann Spak Thal School at Society Hill Synagogue continues to grow and change.

1973: Initiation of the Project

The Ann Spak Thal School was a *shidduh* (match) between a group of parents and a group of rabbinical students who were, from their different perspectives, dissatisfied with the conventional Conservative afternoon Hebrew school. The year 1973 marked the tail end of a glut of educational reforms that had swept over the public schools in the late sixties and early seventies. Programs in affective education, individualized instruction, and multimedia approaches to learning had been initiated in public schools. The students who eventually enrolled in the Ann Spak Thal School were involved in many of the more progressive schools in the Philadelphia School District. These schools had more than their share of innovative programs.

The parents of these children were aware of the vast discrepancy between their children's experience in public school and that in afternoon Hebrew schools. Why were they so bored with the latter and so excited by the former? Was it part of God's plan for the Jewish people to have parents fight children three times a week about the importance of their Jewish education? The rabbinical students, for their part, were eager to experiment with new approaches. Their own growth as Jewish educators was contingent upon finding an environment with fewer administrative constraints, an environment where they could, indeed, try new ways to teach old traditions. The match of dissatisfied parents with ambitious teachers was nearly perfect.

By 1976, when the curriculum was written, the general educational climate had changed radically. Much of the creative energy of the late sixties and early seventies had either diminished or been deemed ineffective. The new alternative schools in Philadelphia focused on getting "back to basics," and they advocated a no-nonsense approach to discipline. This became a test of the merit of the educational changes initiated at the Ann Spak Thal School. Was there real educational substance to them? Or were they just a Jewish manifestation of an educational fad? The 1976 curriculum addressed the issue of the long range stability of educational innovations.

Institutionalizing Educational Creativity

The very fact that a curriculum—a structured program of learning—is now being written for the school reflects a tension at the heart of all educational experiments. One of the great assets of any new program is its flexibility, its ability to respond to the needs of those it serves. This has led some educators to suggest that any kind of structure superimposed upon the needs of students is inherently bad. They argue for a curriculum based solely on the spontaneous needs of students. "Relevance" is the watchword of such a non-curriculum.[1]

Such an approach, however, belies a serious misunderstanding of the nature of student needs as they intersect with various educational environments. It is true that needs are spontaneous developments. Precisely for that reason, an educator cannot build an entire educational program upon student needs. He/she can be open to working with needs when they do emerge, but cannot simply wait for them to emerge. It would also be daring beyond responsibility to try to build an entire educational program out of the educator's often inaccurate perceptions of what constitutes the students' true needs.

There is a real educational need—empirically verified by the failure of innovative schools that do not take this dimension of planning seriously[2]—for a planned curriculum. The problem is that this planned curriculum is often rigidly conceived and executed. This means that a type of learning based on a teacher's response to the needs of the individual learner and on the communal needs of the Jewish people is lost. The planned curriculum literally squeezes out the potentially emergent curriculum. Teachers become afraid to address these needs when they do emerge because of their fear of falling behind in the race to complete the planned curriculum.

At the Ann Spak Thal School we have tried to avoid the polarization and tension between a planned and an emergent curriculum by conceptualizing our curriculum as an interaction of the two. The basic schedule of the school is geared towards the planned curriculum (which itself had elements of individualized instruction in it). Yet, room is also allowed for flexibility stemming from the needs of individual students, the needs of school and synagogue, and the needs of the Jewish community. The arrows in the diagram below indicate the emergence of these special

---

1. See Neil Postman and Charles Weingartner, "What's Worth Knowing," in *Radical School Reform*, ed. Ronald Gross and Beatrice Gross (New York: Simon and Schuster, 1969).
2. Harry Broudy, *The Real World of the Public Schools*, (New York: Harcourt, Brace, Jovanovich, 1972), Introduction, passim.

needs. The dotted line represents a decision-making buffer. As needs arise, the staff meets to see if those needs can be met within the framework of the school without disrupting the planned curriculum or whether the needs are of sufficient importance to override the planned curriculum. Several illustrations of the dynamics of the decision making buffer follow the diagram.

Planned Curriculum
(subject matter, time allotment, method, sequence)

Hebrew	Prayer	*Parashah*	Theme Group

. . . .

	↑		↑		↑
	Needs of student		Needs of school and synagogue		Needs of Jewish community

Emergent Needs
(curriculum merges spontaneously)

Example: Emergent Need of Students

In a conference, a student relates how he is bothered that the headmaster of his school always calls on him to explain Jewish holidays to his Christian classmates. He feels badly because he cannot always respond adequately. The teacher suggests that perhaps the student can work at Hebrew school on preparing a special program for the next Jewish holiday. This is arranged with the headmaster of the student's school. The student uses time allotted for individual projects, as well as some additional time taken from the planned curriculum, to work on his presentation. The need here was considered sufficiently important to release the student from these activities.

Example: Needs of the Synagogue

A recent bar mitzvah has presented the synagogue with a *mezuzah* as a gift. The dedication ceremony is scheduled during school hours. Time is found to allow the whole school to attend the ceremony by shortening each of three planned periods of instruction by five minutes.

Example: Needs of the School

One student is being teased by others in a cruel way. Not only is this unkind but it also affects the climate for learning in the school. A school-wide meeting is called to discuss the problem in lieu of the regular Hebrew period.

Example: Needs of the Jewish Community

The Kissinger proposal for a peace pact between Egypt and Israel is about to be discussed by Congress. Thirty minutes is squeezed out of the normal schedule in order to talk about the proposal and write letters to congressmen.

The departures from the planned curriculum are intended to accomplish specific goals (a better adjustment in school for the student attending parochial school, a more harmonious climate for human relationships and learning from the class meeting, etc.). An important implicit message also comes out of the process. Obligations which students have towards one another as human beings and as Jews are taken more seriously when they are acted upon as well as talked about.

Age Grouping

The Ann Spak Thal School serves the normal age range of the Conservative afternoon school (approximately ages eight to thirteen). The composition of groups and classes in the school is not determined solely on the basis of chronological age. Some activities allow for a mix of students of different ages, while others are geared to more limited age ranges. Although the details of this arrangement are still being worked out, the staff has come to prefer such a "federated" structure because it is responsive to the intellectual and emotional characteristics of children of different ages and yet allows for opportunities to mix ages fruitfully and to bring the entire school together.

The classic work on the non-graded school in the public domain is *The Non-Graded Elementary School* by Goodlad and Anderson (1958). Their central argument is that a child's chronological age says little about his level of intellectual achievement. Rather than force a child into this artificial chronological mold, they suggest grouping students according to ability levels. Reading and math are the primary areas where this is feasible in the public school. The Thal School follows this example to the extent that Hebrew groups have a mix of different aged children of approximately the same Hebrew competency.

There are other benefits to a flexible age-grouping arrangement. The work of Lawrence Kohlberg and his colleagues in the area of moral development has shown that a child's moral development is greatly stimulated by being exposed to the moral reasoning of a child one stage higher than him/herself.[3] This can happen only to a limited extent when a student hears just the moral reasoning of his immediate peers, who are likely to utilize moral reasoning strategies similar to his/her own. Also lost with rigid age grouping is the promotion of helping behavior between older and younger children. At the Thal School older students often become unofficial teacher's aides to the younger students.

There is also, however, a need for differentiation between specific age groups in the school. The most obvious reason for such differentiation is the different cognitive and social orientation between an eight-year-old and a thirteen-year-old. There is also a motivational issue at stake. Children have a need to see change and growth in their lives in school. They need to see themselves moving somewhere within the structure of the school, growing into more responsibility. This is particularly poignant at the Thal School, where students change neither teachers nor rooms from year to year. Consequently, the staff has added new programs each year for the older students. The balance between age-specific and age-mixed activities in the school is shown below.

Age-Specific	Age-Mixed
Counseling Groups	Hebrew
Shabbat Seder Programs	Assemblies
Retreat Program	School Meetings
Individual Projects	Shabbat Services
Bar/Bat Mitzvah *Hug*	Arts and Crafts

For the staff, some of the most exciting educational moments at the Thal School have come when age-mixed and age-specific activities have been integrated into a single program. The *parashah* program, an example of which is included in the "Jewish Social Studies" section below, perhaps best illustrates the point. The overall feeling created in the school when such integration is achieved is that the school is indeed a community of learners. As in any community, differences ought to be respected and used for the overall benefit of the whole group.

For teachers in the Ann Spak Thal School, the experience of working with different aged children at the same time has highlighted differences

---

3. Richard Hersh, Diane Paolitto, and Joseph Reimer, *Promoting Moral Growth* (New York: Longman Press, 1978), pp. 104-106.

in learning style and competency between younger and older students. It is doubtful whether teachers would have gained this insight in as sharp or as focused a way if students of different ages had not been working together. This has aided teachers as they prepared programs designed for children of specific ages. The following guidelines have proved useful in preparing age-specific programs.

Older children have the following characteristics: they can be given a role in planning; they are socially oriented to their peer group; they are capable of imaginative role-playing; they take the bar and bat mitzvah ceremonies seriously; they possess a budding ability to deal with abstractions; they can carry out a project independently; and they require a longer period of time to get involved. By contrast, younger children are skills-oriented and product-oriented; they have shorter attention spans; they adopt a literal approach to role-playing; and they have a greater need for the presence and supervision of teachers.

Jewish Social Studies

The Scope of the Program

The "Jewish Social Studies" section of the curriculum consists of five broad areas. They are: 1) Jewish History; 2) Jewish Personalities; 3) Israel; 4) Jews Around the World; and 5) Jewish Creativity and Civilization. Each of these broad areas becomes the focus for the weekday school sessions of the Thal School for approximately six weeks each year. Students become integrated into the theme for the six weeks by choosing an area of specialization from among those activities offered by teachers. Materials-making and special projects in the school during this six-week period are all geared to the general theme.

There are five themes within each of the five broad areas of the Jewish Social Studies curriculum. One theme is offered each year. Thus, at the end of five years all the major themes within each area have been covered. By the time a student has finished five years at the school he/she has been involved in each of the themes listed below. This satisfies the important curricular criterion of proper scope of study. The staff feels that this curriculum insures that students will be exposed to the widest possible variety of facets of Judaism and Jewish life in the course of their years at the school.

Revolving Five-Year Jewish Social Studies Program

The group topics listed after each main theme below are suggested ones. Others may be added or substituted in the course of the faculty's planning of the theme groups. Care should be taken, however, to maintain the scope of the curriculum, so that all theme areas are covered over the course of the student's five years in the school.

Israel
Theme #1: History of Israel: Pre-1948
    1. Rise of Zionism   2. The experiences of early *halutzim*
3. *Aliyot*   4. Rebirth of the Hebrew language   5. Political problems: *Haganah, Irgun,* Jewish-Arab relations

Theme #2: History of Israel: Post-1948
    1. Events immediately surrounding the establishment of the State of Israel   2. Government of Israel   3. Wars since independence
4. Early problems of the state: absorption of new immigrants, defense, etc.

Theme #3: People of Israel
    1. Sephardic Jews   2. Kibbutz life   3. American *olim*   4. Israeli minorities   5. Religious and non-religious lifestyles   6. Costumes of Israel

Theme #4: Geography of Israel
    1. Rebuilding of the Land   2. Modern Israel as compared to biblical Israel   3. Jerusalem: old and new   4. Important cities
5. Beautiful natural sites

Theme #5: Life and Culture of Israel
    1. Children of Israel   2. Art and music of Israel   3. Israeli stamps and coins   4. Israeli sports and recreation   5. Israeli foods
6. Holidays in Israel

Jewish History
Theme #1: Biblical Life
    1. Leaders in biblical times   2. Magic and superstition in the Bible   3. Biblical crafts   4. Archaeology of biblical times

Theme #2: American-Jewish History
    1. Waves of immigration to America   2. The Lower East Side
3. Philadelphia Jewish history   4. Different types of Jewish observance in America

Theme #3: The Rabbinic Period of Jewish History
    1. The Second Temple   2. Dead Sea Scrolls   3. Masada

Theme #4: Holocaust
    1. History of European Jews just before the Holocaust   2. Jewish resistance   3. Concentration camps   4. Literature of survivors

Theme #5: Jews in Eastern Europe
    1. *Shtetl* life   2. Yiddish literature   3. Synagogues of Eastern Europe   4. Hasidism 5. Magic and superstition

Jews Around the World
Theme #1: Soviet Jews
   1. Refuseniks   2. History of Jews in Russia   3. Letter-writing
campaign   4. Freedom songs of Soviet Jews

Theme #2: Customs of Jews around the World
   1. Ethiopian Jews   2. Sephardic customs   3. Samaritans
4. Jews in Asia   5. Special Israeli customs   6. Different languages
and dress of Jews

Theme #3: Jews in Trouble
   1. Jews in Arab lands   2. Rescue operations in Jewish history
(e.g., Operation Magic Carpet)   3. Poor Jews in America 4. Dying
Jewish communities

Theme #4: American Jews Today

Theme #5: Responsibility of Jews for One Another

Jewish Creativity and Civilization
Theme #1: Folktales
   1. Wise Men of Helm   2. Hasidic tales   3. Folktales of Israel
4. Yiddish folktales   5. Myths of the Bible

Theme #2: Jewish Ethics
   1. *Pirke Avot*   2. *Bet Din* (Jewish court)   3. *Tzedakah*   4. Ten
Commandments

Theme #3: Jewish Law
   1. Laws of Shabbat   2. Laws concerning relations between "man
and man"   3. *Kashrut* laws

Theme #4: Jewish Art and Music
   1. Modern Israeli music   2. Ritual art   3. Synagogue architecture   4. *Haggadot* and *Megillot*

Theme #5: Jewish Foods
   1. Eastern European foods   2. *Kashrut* laws   3. Israeli foods
4. Holiday foods

Jewish Personalities
Theme #1: American-Jewish Personalities
   1. Jews in American history   2. Jews in sports   3. Jews in enter-
tainment   4. Jews in politics and law   5. What does it mean to be
a Jew in America?

Theme #2: Biblical Heroes
   1. Famous biblical women   2. Prophets   3. Patriarchs
4. Biblical villains

Theme #3: Famous Rabbis
    1. Akiba   2. Maimonides   3. Hillel   4. Baal Shem Tov
    5. Vilna Gaon   6. Rashi   7. Solomon Schechter   8. Stephen Wise
    9. The Lubavitcher Rebbe

Theme #4: Zionist Heroes
    1. Theodore Herzl   2. David Ben-Gurion   3. Chaim Weitz-
mann   4. Golda Meir   5. Henrietta Szold   6. Hannah Senesh
    7. Mickey Marcus

Theme #5: Jews in Arts and Sciences
    1. Albert Einstein   2. Marc Chagall   3. Sholom Aleichem
    4. Ben Shahn

The Question of Student Motivation

"Jewish Social Studies" is the area of the Thal curriculum that demands
most of a teacher's Jewish knowledge and his/her educational creativity.
In most afternoon Hebrew schools, this section of the curriculum is taught
through textbooks. At the Thal School, the staff has developed procedures for teaching theme groups through teacher-generated instructional
strategies. As mentioned before, students are allowed to choose from a
number of alternative group projects, all related to the central theme. This
procedure is not uncommon in Jewish schools for junior high school students. It is extremely rare, however, at the elementary level. It will further illuminate the educational philosophy of the school and the staff's
understanding of working with American Jewish children to explain this
departure from the norm.

    "Jewish Social Studies" has an entirely different relationship to a stu-
dent's life than do the other sections of the curriculum. The reading of
Hebrew is a skill. It can be appreciated by most children through the same
excitement they experience when mastering any new task. The
experiences described in the "Jewish Life" section of the curriculum have
an aesthetic and spiritual value which is integral to the continued survival of Jewish holidays and sancta. The material in this section of the
curriculum, however, has neither of these connections with students'
lives.

    American Jewish children, at least as they are typified at the Thal
School, live in a cultural milieu which is primarily non-Jewish. The most
significant consequence of this situation is that the personalities, events,
and values (the essence of any social studies curriculum, Jewish or secular)
of the general culture have a much greater resonance for children than
do the corresponding personalities, events, and values of Jewish culture.
Batman and the date of the American Revolution have a greater hold on

American Jewish children's minds and imaginations than do Moses and the date of the destruction of the Second Temple.

Under these conditions, it is unrealistic to expect a child to pick up a Jewish textbook (even some of the better new ones) and begin reading with any real enthusiasm. The material is likely to seem flat in tone and hollow in resonance. This often has little to do with the merit of the text—the author may have done his or her job quite well. But the reader, the young Jewish child, cannot respond adequately. The requisite chain of associations and responses—his or her Jewish literacy—is missing.

In these circumstances, the continued use of conventional means of social studies—reading, discussing, and analyzing—becomes a repetition of what Paul Tillich has called the fatal pedagogic error—namely, throwing answers like stones at the heads of people who have yet to ask the questions.[4]

The response of many Hebrew schools when faced with this lack of internally generated student motivation has been to press hard with more external motivation (discipline, guilt about not caring about Judaism, etc.). On the whole, this strategy has not yielded adequate results in terms of students' intellectual achievements. It has also contributed to the negative feelings which students often have about their Jewish education.

The solution attempted at the Thal School is of a different sort. In broad outline, it follows a suggestion by George Brown in *Human Teaching for Human Learning*. Brown traces Tillich's "fatal pedagogic error" to the curricular tendency to compress and organize knowledge to such a degree that it bears little relation to the original human experience it describes. The key to making this knowledge come alive for children is to restore the knowledge to its original human context.[5] The approach is also congruent with Piaget's insight that, while seven- to twelve-year-olds can deal with ideas, they must deal with them in their concrete expression in human life, rather than in their abstract place in the academic arrangement of disciplined knowledge.[6] Described below is an extended example of how the staff attempted to employ the approach suggested by Brown during a *parashah* program. As indicated earlier, it also is an example of how age-specific and mixed-age activities are integrated in the school.

Parashah Presentation: Jacob's Wrestling Match

In *Parashat Va-Yishlah*, the encounter of Jacob with the messenger of God

---

4. George Brown, *Human Teaching for Human Learning* (New York: Viking Press, 1971).
5. Ibid.
6. Jean Piaget, *Six Psychological Studies* (New York: Random House, 1968), p. 47f.

and his subsequent name change are described. The presentation to students of the *parashah* program followed these lines. During the Torah section of our Shabbat service, four key lines from the story were read. A brief orientation to the *parashah* and a review of the events in Jacob's life in the previous two *parashiyot* were given through a *D'var Torah*.

The major educational activity related to the *parashah* came later in the day. Students assembled as a school. The teachers prepared a simulation in which one of them is thinking about cheating on an exam. Two other teachers, one assuming the role of his *yetzer ha-tov* (good inclination) and the other assuming the role of his *yetzer ha-ra* (evil inclination), sat at each side.

An appropriate sign made it clear that the two *yetzarim* represent the different sides of a person's conscience. Each offered reasons why the teacher should or should not cheat. Students were then invited into the simulation to talk about which *yetzer* they might follow were they in that situation. It was then related to the group that some Jewish and non-Jewish commentators on the Bible have suggested that the messenger represents a struggle within Jacob's own conscience. The school was then divided into three smaller groups. The youngest group was given the task of talking about some situation where they had felt torn between their own *yetzer ha-tov* and *yetzer ha-ra*. They were also asked to prepare a skit about such a situation for the school. The middle group was given a list of people who, like Jacob, had changed their names (mostly Jewish but some non-Jewish—David Green to David Ben-Gurion, Avram to Avraham, Cassius Clay to Muhammad Ali). They were to explore the reason why each of these individuals had changed his name. The oldest group was asked to discuss name changes in a more general way. Could changing a name change the way you feel about yourself? What's the significance of a name? There was also a brief discussion of the name changes of many Jewish families when they immigrated to America.

The smaller groups reassembled and shared with one another what they had talked about. A teacher then attempted to summarize the importance of Jacob's wrestling with the angel and his subsequent change of names by asking students to help her reorder the events of Jacob's life, which were listed on a chart. This helped them to see that the change in Jacob's name was also related to a change in character, which could be verified by looking at the things which Jacob did before and after he wrestled with the messenger.

Several things about the presentation are worth noting. First, it attempted to explore the biblical incident through the human dimensions inherent in the story and situation. But it also attempted to avoid the pitfalls of that approach when put into a Jewish setting. Something uniquely Jewish was also happening to Jacob. Attention was paid at both the beginning and the end to the unique context of these events in the biblical narrative and the underlying assumptions that shaped the biblical view of the world. There was also an implicit awareness (one which should be made quite explicit at a later point) between *peshat* (the direct meaning of the text) and *derash* (interpretation). Finally, attention was paid to the different levels at which children could approach the text. Ten-year-olds (the middle group) could talk about name changes in a relatively concrete manner. But to have spoken with them about names in a more abstract way (as was done with the twelve-year-olds) would not have been very fruitful.

The approach outlined above in the *parashah* presentation requires staff who both are gifted teachers and have a thorough understanding of the dynamics of the Jewish tradition. It presupposes teachers who are sufficiently familiar and comfortable with the various structures of Jewish experience and thought to abstract the major concepts and relate them to children's lives. It requires, in short, a dressing in Jewish garb of Jerome Bruner's contention that any concept can be taught to a child of any age in some intellectually honest way.

The second distinguishing feature of the Thal School's approach to student motivation within the "Jewish Social Studies Curriculum" is the element of student choice allowed in each theme group. This is the other side of the teacher's feeling of "ownership" of the curriculum when he or she has helped develop it. When students are given a framework that allows them to choose from among clearly stated alternatives, they feel some "ownership" of the curriculum, too. This does not solve all motivational problems. Among other things, some students simply end up choosing the group they dislike least. The experience of the Thal staff, however, is that it has been an important element in the extremely positive attitude which students have towards the school.

Also at work here is the notion that different students do indeed have different "learning styles." Standard curricula strive to create experiences that make demands and offer rewards for students in many different media. It is thought that each student can approach a subject through intellectual discussion, music, drama, etc. Each of these media has a place within the string of experiences prescribed for every student. The staff of the Thal School, however, accepts the notion that students (like human beings in general) are simply not that versatile. Students do have different interests, abilities, and competencies. In creating theme groups, a deliberate attempt is made to provide a balance between the activities students will be asked to choose.

"Jewish Social Studies": Procedures and Structures for Theme Groups

Listed below are some of the procedures and structures which have developed as part of teaching theme groups. What should be obvious is the enormous amount of teacher effort required to replace a "textbook" curriculum with one developed by teachers working with one another.

Staff Meetings

At least a week prior to the beginning of a theme group, a faculty meeting is held. A particular emphasis of the meeting is brainstorming about the richest possible assortment of offerings related to the theme. Attention is also given to establishing a common set of goals for the theme group and assigning responsibilities for the development of individualized materials that can be used to reinforce the material taught in theme groups.

Student Introduction to Theme Groups

The first day on which a theme group begins, students choose their activity for the six weeks. This is facilitated by a twenty-minute period in which small groups of students visit each staff member to see what he/she will be offering. At the end of that period, students choose the two groups they prefer to join. Students are assigned to one of their two choices.

Tzedakah

For a complete discussion of the Thal School's approach to *tzedakah*, see the section on theme groups in the essay, "Doing Justice to *Tzedakah*," in this volume.

Audio-Visual

On Shabbat, a movie or filmstrip is shown which relates to the theme group.

Discussion Questions

At the beginning of each weekday session, students meet in small groups and receive an orientation to the day. During this time one particular feeling connected to the theme group is talked about in a personal way.

For example, during the study of the *Yishuv* (pre-1948 Jewish community in Palestine), the Hebrew word for the day was *halutz* (pioneer). In the orientation groups, students talked about how they would feel being part of the return of the Jewish people to their land and facing the hardships there.

Board Games

The Thal School has a large supply of teacher-designed board games. For each theme group, two teachers take the responsibility for developing a game incorporating the content of that theme group.

Arts and Crafts

Some short projects related to the theme group are prepared for use at the beginning and end of the school days. Music related to the theme group is sometimes introduced on Shabbat.

A Learning Model for Jewish Education

It was suggested at the beginning of this article that the appropriateness of secular learning models for Jewish education should be treated as an open question, a matter of ongoing experimentation. In the course of preparing this curriculum, the staff came to appreciate that one particular model of the learning process best explained the experience of the staff over the three years in which it worked with provisional models and without a formal curriculum. It is the information-processing model developed by Terry Borton.[7]

Borton suggests that we look at the process of acquiring new knowledge in the following way:

Activity	Question Asked
Acting	Now what?
Transforming	So what?
Sensing	What?

This model implies that information must start at the sensory level and move through the transforming and acting levels. Only then is the information processed completely and the full educational value of the

---

7. Terry Borton and Norm Newberg, *Education for Student Concerns* (Philadelphia: Philadelphia School District, 1972), pp. 6-10.

material gleaned. The guide for moving through these different levels is the particular question the student asks at each level. At the sensing level, students orient themselves to what is being presented. They experience and intuit meaning. They ask "what" is going on. At the transforming level, students begin assigning intellectual and emotional significance to the information. They work it into broader cognitive and affective frameworks. The person asks the question, "So what?" Why is the information important? At the third level, the students begin to question what they are to do with the information they now understand. What difference does the knowledge make for the person's actions? How can he/she express in a concrete and significant way the knowledge he/she has acquired?

By and large, Jewish curricula have oriented themselves to the second level of transformation, the "so what?" level. This approach in isolation misses the crucial integration of knowledge into the lower and higher levels. In relation to the "sensing—what?" level, the conventional approach makes the mistaken assumption that the students are already oriented to the material being presented. Without the initial sensory/experiential involvements, students will not be ready to assign intellectual and personal significance to the new material learned. With regard to the "acting—now what?" level of Borton's model, standard Jewish curricula do not usually help students bridge the gap between what they might know and the kinds of things which can convert that knowledge into ethical action. According to Borton, when the sensing and acting levels are neglected, information may not even be assimilated at the "transforming—so what?" level that is the explicit goal of the curriculum.

The staff at the Thal School has tried to provide connections for most of the things taught at all three levels of Borton's model. It was mentioned before that the "Jewish Life" section of the curriculum (particularly through the Shabbat Seder program, described elsewhere in this volume) attempts to acquaint students with the sounds, smells, and tastes of Shabbat. This is the basic level of sensing and experiencing a holiday which a student must go through before being prepared to ask questions about that tradition's significance. Many of the educational games utilized in the school for theme groups serve the function of catching the student's eye and providing basic information before going on to the more intensive questioning which occurs in theme groups.

The staff has also made provisions for insuring that students move from the transforming level of studying in theme groups to some level of "acting—now what?" in Borton's model. For instance, at the end of each theme group, a class meeting is held. One of the things decided at that meeting is what to do with the tzedakah raised during the six weeks of theme group. Three options, all connected to the theme being studied, are suggested. Students discuss the merits of each and finally vote on which organization should receive the money. The theme group on Soviet Jewry one year extended the acting dimension of their learning even further. Some students went with a teacher and bought a number of items which were then sent to refuseniks in the Soviet Union.

In general, the experience of the staff has been that paying attention to these levels of sensing and acting, which are often ignored, has not only enriched instruction in the school but has also given our students at least as much pure information as students in other Hebrew schools. The Borton model has become a useful way of making sure that the process of teaching and learning Jewish material accords with the patterns which, researchers in education suggest, allow human beings to function at their fullest potential. It is probably beyond the capacity of any school staff to insure that each new learning experience provides for a well thought out movement through the three dimensions of sensing, transforming, and acting. Yet, the lack of attention that has been given to these dimensions of the learning process may account for some of the persistent learning and motivation problems which students who are known to be capable in the non-Jewish segment of their learning encounter in Jewish educational institutions.

A Breath of Fresh Learning

■ ■ ■ David Brusin and Cynthia Toback

Afternoon religious schools are universally censured by Jewish educators and laymen alike. They are judged educationally suspect for various reasons, though the following are typical: they involve too few hours of instruction to be effective at the outset; there is virtually no support or reinforcement at home; part-time instructors are uninterested and untrained; full-time teachers are overworked and underpaid and are often recruited from the public or day schools. How easy it is to relieve ourselves of responsibility. We continually describe and lament what is "given," over which we have little control, thereby implying that circumstances, rather than ourselves, are to blame for the failure of the educational enterprise in which we are engaged.

Our attention and energies should instead be directed toward seeking ways to counteract such negative conditions. There is, in fact, a great deal that can be done to make the afternoon religious school a more congenial and effective place of Jewish learning, caring, and commitment. Indeed, the possibilities are endless. One such response is the creation of a paradigmatic learning environment within the synagogue school that can be closely monitored and controlled. We believe that the introduction of a Learning Center, along the lines discussed below, can provide an important step toward this goal.

Educational Bearings

The Learning Center we established in our school was motivated by pragmatic as well as theoretical concerns. Ideally, we wanted to reinforce and complement the ongoing, overall curriculum of our school through a variety of teaching techniques, such as individualized study programs, fine arts projects, holiday- and history-related games, and the like. We realized, too, that such enrichments should emerge directly from the formal curriculum and, at the same time, be relatively uniform from year to year within each grade level. Practically speaking, not all teachers are disposed or equipped to introduce multi-media or special crafts projects into their classrooms. Yet it is also true that students benefit from an exposure to a variety of teaching approaches and personalities, regardless of the limited time frame within which we operate.

With this in mind, we inaugurated a Learning Center in the fall of 1977 for *alef* classes alone. An additional grade was added each subsequent year so that, as of September 1981, all classes from *alef* through *heih* visit the Center for one hour a week out of a total of six, or six and a half hours in the case of *daled* and *heih*. Student response has been overwhelmingly positive and encouraging. Curriculum coordination between the director of the Learning Center and the religious school faculty has stabilized over the last three years. Teachers now know the scope and specific content of projects undertaken in the Center. This, in turn, allows the faculty to emphasize other aspects of Jewish history and festival instruction in their lessons. Students, for their part, are more inclined to engage in serious textual study in class, having experienced the informal, affective learning that goes on in the Learning Center each week. We look forward to the time when, funding permitting, the Center will be open and supervised during all the hours that our school is in session. It would then be possible for some classes to visit the Center more than once a week.

The Learning Center is likewise beginning to have a significant impact on what takes place in the classroom itself. Over the years, a virtual gold mine of supplementary teaching materials and educational aids has been prepared. Our staff is gradually discovering how to utilize these educational resources at other times during the week, both in and out of the Center. A specific game designed for use in the Learning Center in connection with a particular holiday or subject can be introduced in the classroom with students who need additional reinforcement. This can provide the teacher a precious few moments to work with individuals or small groups of students. Teachers greatly appreciate the added flexibility which the existence of such materials affords them.

Personnel and Finances

One critical factor in the development and operation of a Learning Center should be stressed at the outset: personnel. The director of the Learning Center must be well versed in the entire range of audio-visual hardware and software, yet equally at home with more traditional materials — crayons and construction paper, for instance. The Learning Center director must conceive and carry out programs for children ranging in age from eight to thirteen, whose artistic levels of interest and ability differ widely. Clearly, not everyone with the requisite academic qualifications is capable of administering such a diverse program, with its several distinct stages of planning and execution, particularly in the context of a Jewish school. At the same time, the Learning Center director must be able to work with a variety of teachers, since the classroom teacher accompanies his or her class to the Center.

Without a competent and highly creative director—one who will not hesitate to prepare detailed lesson plans, as well as mountains of dittos and board games—a Learning Center is not very likely to succeed. An open classroom, a true *center of learning*, seeks to eliminate the inherent restrictions and limitations that the traditional learning environment imposes. Yet, perhaps somewhat paradoxically, the internal structure and design of a Learning Center that functions properly is patently more complex, more elaborate, and more demanding in terms of planning and preparation—in short, more rigorously conceived and organized than its "traditional" counterpart. For this reason alone, the success of a Learning Center is far more dependent on personnel than would otherwise be the case. Content and subject usually speak for themselves. In a Learning Center, the very task at hand is to create a project, game, or subject-student encounter that itself supplies the means for addressing and challenging the participant in a predetermined manner. The medium may not be the message in its entirety, but it plays a peculiar and complex role in the transmission process. Consequently, the construction of the vehicle of transmission in a Learning Center requires a special kind of individual, for in this setting the instructor and the vehicle presented interact in unique ways. In the same sense that we would not expect every teacher to be capable of writing a textbook, we cannot expect every teacher to be able to create, *ab initio*, and to direct, *ad infinitum*, a Learning Center serving a broad spectrum of subjects, students, and objectives.

Budget is never easy to estimate, especially given present economic uncertainties. Twelve hundred dollars for every hour the Center is in operation constitutes a rough guideline for salary, hardware and software, and miscellaneous operating costs. Some equipment will be available at the start; some—individualized language systems, for example—may not be realizable at all. A Center need not do everything at once. It may well be decided at the outset to limit its objectives for whatever reasons—financial or otherwise. The existence of a community-based Teacher's Center, such as the Kohl Jewish Teacher Center (in Wilmette, Illinois), can simplify the initial challenge faced by the creation of an in-house Learning Center; it can also greatly expand the latter's potential where funds or ideas are lacking.

Underlying Assumptions and Objectives

Examples of projects developed in our Learning Center, described below, indicate how we have begun to tap the potential that exists within this learning model. Similar techniques and projects can be, and surely are, found in other frames of reference, including more typical classroom settings. Our efforts to establish a five year curriculum in a Learning Center have proved worthwhile so far. And the concept itself has proved to be a breath of fresh learning in our afternoon school. Students and teachers attest to this daily. We are therefore optimistic about what might be achieved in the long run, both in our own school and elsewhere.

The operating educational philosophy of our Learning Center is no different than that of effective teacher-subject dynamics in the broadest sense. A good teacher, employing sound teaching techniques, attempts to evoke a positive response to the subject being explored in the life and mind of the student. As always, teacher-student rapport is a crucial element in the scheme. Still, the Learning Center itself must be recognized as an additional, experiential component that affects the process in a unique fashion. Whereas positive teacher-student rapport is impossible to program (though essential), the imposed structure of the Learning Center can more readily be studied, understood, and manipulated. Control and direction from the outside can more easily be appraised here.

The underlying purpose of our Learning Center is also very simply stated: to promote enthusiasm for, and interest in, religious school in particular, and Judaism in general, by providing a relaxed and stimulating environment in which students can have positive Jewish learning experiences. The Center accomplishes its central aim by furnishing intellectual, emotional, tactile, and creative learning opportunities through various projects or units. Accordingly, each unit of instruction includes a variety of activities, a series of options, in order to appeal to different levels of interest, ability, and motivation within each age group. In the *alef* year (eight-year-olds), the emphasis is visual and tactile, with an overall arts and crafts orientation. The *bet* and *gimel* years involve considerably more cognitive learning options, while the *daled* and *heih* years incorporate numerous long term study and research projects. There is always a manipulative, audio-visual or craft activity associated with any given unit of instruction.

The Physical Setting

Our Learning Center is permanently housed in a large classroom with several six-foot tables and chairs for group seating, open shelves with arts and crafts materials, plus an extensive assortment of games, individualized study units, and puzzles. A closet was transformed into a study carrel and two long walls provide adequate bulletin board and blackboard space. Students are responsible for the care of the materials and the general condition of the Center after each session. Since there is no grading or reporting procedure, a point system was devised for additional motivation. Each part of a unit is assigned a point value; every few months points are totaled and prizes awarded to the top three students in each class. An ongoing record of each student's points is posted on one of the bulletin boards.

Curricular Examples

The *alef* year begins with an extended unit, consisting of several sessions, on the synagogue. Early in the unit, students take a guided tour of the building, focusing on the various offices (those of the rabbi, cantor, principal, executive director), the cantor's music room, the *bet midrash*, our synagogue's Jewish museum, *simhah* wall,* and stained glass window, the memorial alcove, the main sanctuary, *bimah*, *sifrei torah*, etc. Students are introduced to the people connected with these areas, and the role each plays in the functioning of the synagogue is explained and discussed. Returning to the Learning Center, students are asked to compose questions about what they have seen and heard. These questions then serve as the basis for a team game of tic-tac-toe. The project that follows offers a choice of activities: a mural-sized picture of the sanctuary, a diorama of the sanctuary using shoe boxes or cardboard, or a mural-sized map of either level of the synagogue. Related projects include: teacher-prepared tic-tac-toe games, a synagogue word search, taped interviews with students role-playing, and a filmstrip on the synagogue shown to the class as a whole or on individual viewers in the study carrels. Besides producing some very fine artwork that is shared with parents, the unit helps to familiarize students with the objects of central importance in the synagogue. More importantly, it introduces *alef* students, at the very beginning of their religious school education, to the synagogue building itself and to the people whose lives revolve around it.

A number of sessions in the *bet* year are devoted to a study of Hasidism. The unit opens with a filmstrip of old Jerusalem followed by a discussion of the mode of dress, religious observance, and history of the Hasidic movement. Activities include: coloring or cutting pictures of

---

* A sculpture in the form of an *Etz Hayim* where leaves or rocks are purchased in honor of congregants' *simhot*.

Hasidim for drawings or collages; worksheets based on the books *Tradition: Orthodox Life in America* (Mal Warshaw, Schocken Books, New York, 1976) and *The Face of Faith: A Chasidic Community* (George Kranzler, Baltimore Hebrew College Press, Baltimore, 1972); a discussion of the song "Tradition" from *Fiddler on the Roof;* a comparison of the Hasidic lifestyle with our own and that of our parents and grandparents.

An extensive unit on Jewish roots (six to eight sessions) was organized for the *gimel* (or *daled*) year. Our primary source, the Skokie telephone directory, is distributed in class, along with a Jewish roots question sheet that includes, for example: How many synagogues are there in Skokie? What are the denominations represented? How many kosher butcher shops are there in Skokie? Is there a Jewish hospital in Skokie? How many people have the same last name as you?

A personal history sheet then follows. Students (along with their parents, of course) are expected to discover the answers to such questions as: Where were your grandparents born? When and how did they come to America? What kind of work did they do when they first settled here? Where do your aunts, uncles, grandparents live now? When the students return these sheets, the countries of origin are plotted on a large wall map along with present geographic locations. The unit concludes with a discussion and worksheet on Jewish names.

Activities for the final project include a family tree, a family time line, a mobile with family pictures and heirlooms, a taped interview with a grandparent, a written account of the history of a family member as told to the student, a unit on immigration, and an examination of Jewish social services (such as HIAS and Jewish Vocational Guidance) available in the Chicago Metropolitan area. In this way, we are able to present a perspective on the origins of American Jewish life that pertains directly to the life of the student.

The *daled* curriculum includes a survey of Jewish history from biblical times to the present. To augment the textbook study, two units, requiring six to eight sessions each, were created for the Center. One concentrates on Jewish personalities of the nineteenth and twentieth centuries. Students begin by compiling a list of well-known Jews in the arts, politics, sports, science, and medicine. Thirty packets have been prepared so far, containing short biographies of famous Jewish personalities of the last two centuries along with questions for discussion, both subjective and factual. Filmstrips, records, poems, and other information are presented regularly. Each student is required to become familiar with one personality in particular and, eventually, to report to the class on that individual. The unit culminates with a bingo board game on all the individuals studied.

The second supplement to the *daled* survey of Jewish history is a unit on the kibbutz. Following the presentation of basic information, including some discussion of what life on a kibbutz is like, students elect kibbutz officers and central committee members. They then hold kibbutz meetings for the first fifteen minutes of class. Conflict situations are provided to heighten student sensitivity and understanding of kibbutz life, such as issues of shared housing, of salary increases, and of the need for medical attention outside the kibbutz. A diorama of a kibbutz is the art project of the unit, with small groups of students responsible for particular sections of the whole. The unit terminates on or close to *Yom Ha'atzmaut* with a "real" celebration—food, games and dancing.

Many other similarly conceived units have been developed. To mention a few: a values-clarification exercise for Shavuot, involving a ranking of the *asseret ha-dibrot* and the formulation of a "modern" version of the same; appropriately decorated T-shirts for the annual (Greater Chicago) Walk with Israel; a dramatic presentation of the *shofar*, rehearsed and performed just prior to Rosh Hashanah by *heih* classes; handmade *ketubot* in conjunction with a unit on marriage; handmade *mezuzot* in the context of a unit on the Jewish home; a biblical scavenger hunt for *alef* students on *Lag B'omer*; and the performance of a play based on the life of Golda Meir as part of a unit on Zionism and Israel for *gimel* students.

It is seldom possible to know beforehand how the weekly visits to the Learning Center will be integrated into the general, formal curriculum for each grade over the course of the year. This integration, crucial as it is, cannot be programmed in advance. It must evolve naturally and experientially, based on trial and error and mutual trust. In our case, where the Learning Center director and the entire faculty (eight in number) have remained constant over the last six years, this trust has grown steadily during weekly encounters in the Center and at regular (as well as spontaneous) staff meetings. Sharing of ideas and mutual cooperation are plainly the crux of the matter. Since the classroom teacher accompanies the class to the Center, integration should not be viewed as an obstacle to be overcome all at once. It is, rather, a question of fitting the pieces together, allowing space for flexibility and movement in all directions. The longer the process continues, it now appears to us, the greater and the more productive the interaction, integration, and interdependence between the Learning Center and the classroom.

A Final Plea

Establishing and maintaining a Learning Center obviously requires a great deal of time and planning. The return, in terms of student, parent, and staff enthusiasm, has convinced us that it is well worth the effort and the expense. More than anything else, the religious school must strive to inculcate and at the same time represent within its walls our concern for and connection with the larger Jewish community — K'lal Yisrael. This must be accomplished experientially as well as cognitively if it is to have a long-range effect on the lives of our students. The afternoon religious school can provide this kind of experience in the context of a Learning Center. It is our belief that children can thereby begin to feel our love for Judaism and for them.

Teaching About
Other Religions

■ ■ ■ Nancy Fuchs-Kreimer

Mordecai Kaplan, after making *aliyah* to Israel, expressed the wish that he be buried in the United States.[1] This gesture symbolizes Reconstructionism's unique contribution to Jewish thought. As the only movement in Jewish life to be conceived in and for the American scene, Reconstructionism insists on recognizing the American situation as a radically new challenge, unprecedented in Jewish history. The "classical" Reconstructionist position concerning other religions is deeply indebted to this recognition. In the last several decades, important changes in America have seriously challenged that position. Much of its insight, however, endures—more needed now than ever. This becomes clear when one explores the implications of the classical Reconstructionist position on Jewish education.

Educational issues are crucial. In order to decide where and what we are willing to teach our children, we must make judgments about the shape of the world in which we live. This chapter will present an updated Reconstructionist approach to the setting and content of learning about other religions. Two specific plans are offered: one attempts to address the issue of public vs. parochial education through the idea of a model school. The other deals with what might be taught about other religions in a course for Jewish adolescents. The judgments on which these ideas

---

1. Private conversation with Rabbi Ira Eisenstein, December, 1979.

are based are provisional, the plans hypothetical. They are intended to stimulate alternative judgments, more creativity, and further "reconstruction."

I. PUBLIC VS. PAROCHIAL SCHOOLING

Classical Position

The classical Reconstructionist position involves a strong commitment to public education. To appreciate fully that commitment, one must understand the theory upon which it rests. For Reconstructionists, American Jews live in two civilizations, both of which are religious and neither of which contradicts the other. Before Robert Bellah popularized the concept of civil religion,[2] Kaplan had written extensively on the "faith of America" and the "religion of democracy." Because he was a follower of Durkheim, Kaplan was quick to notice, as Bellah did later, that American civilization was not without its religious component. As Robin Williams wrote, "Every functioning society has...a common religion. The possession of a common set of ideas, rituals and symbols can supply an overarching sense of unity even in a society riddled with conflict."[3] The American flag, the Constitution, the Fourth of July, and Thanksgiving are only a few of the sancta that Kaplan understood to be the concrete expressions of the American faith, belonging to no particular denomination, but binding together most Americans in a spiritual way.

Reconstructionism has argued that the civil religion of America is a positive phenomenon for Jews. For Reconstructionists, there is nothing about America that prevents the development of Judaism, and nothing about Judaism that makes it impossible to be a good American. As Reconstructionist thinker Milton Steinberg put it, "Lincoln and Jefferson are my heroes together with Rabbi Akiba and Moses Maimonides. The four get along in my imagination most companionably."[4] This mutually fructifying situation is possible because America is, by its nature, committed to pluralism. Kaplan recognizes that it is not always or even usually possible to live easily in two civilizations. For example, he argues that it would be impossible to be both a Jew and a Christian because the two civiliza-

2. Robert Bellah, "Civil Religion in America," *Daedalus* 96 (1967):1. See also Sidney Mead, "The Nation with the Soul of a Church," *Church History* 36 (1967):262.
3. Robin Williams, *American Society: A Sociological Interpretation* (New York: Alfred Knopf, 1952), p. 312.
4. Milton Steinberg, *A Believing Humanism* (New York: Harcourt, Brace and Co., 1951), p. 98.

tions are contradictory.[5] In the case of American religion, however, the highest ideals of our country are seen as compatible with Judaism and thus the two are complementary in nature.

In 1951, Kaplan and several colleagues published *The Faith of America*, a collection of readings, songs, and prayers for the celebration of American holy days.[6] As recently as 1976, Ira Eisenstein defended civil religion against its detractors, writing, "There is more to be gained than lost from a truly ethical 'faith of America.'"[7]

Jewish youth, in such a view, need to be socialized in and contribute to the common life of the nation. The public school system of America has served as the "church" of the civil faith, and Jews, especially Reconstructionists, have traditionally been committed to that system. As Kaplan wrote, "A Jewish parochial school system would be but a futile gesture of protest against the necessity of giving Jewish civilization a position ancillary to the civilization of the majority."[8] The assumption is that public schools could train children to be moral citizens and human beings through the values of the civil religion. Kaplan urged that the history and culture of American democracy be taught in the public schools in a religious spirit.[9] To the extent that youth need to know about their neighbors' beliefs to function in a pluralistic society, they could gain such information through objective courses *about* religion in the public school.[10] Finally, Jewish civilization could be inculcated at home and through supplementary education, including, for Kaplan, all manner of Jewish communal life. Such a combination of public and Jewish education would admirably prepare Jewish children to become part of American life in a setting of healthy civil religion and pluralism.

Since the classical position was formulated, however, America has undergone radical changes, few of which were foreseen. There are forces at work in contemporary America which make us wonder whether the classical position was designed for a situation which no longer exists. Our challenge is to create a Reconstructionist approach to the new situation as we understand it.

---

5. Mordecai Kaplan, *Judaism as a Civilization* (New York: Reconstructionist Press, 1951), p.305.
6. Kaplan, Williams, and Kohn, *The Faith of America* (New York: Reconstructionist Press, 1951).
7. Ira Eisenstein, "Is the U.S. Ready for a Civil Religion?" *The Philadelphia Inquirer*, reprinted in *Religious Education* 71 (1976):227.
8. Mordecai Kaplan, *Judaism as a Civilization*, p. 489.
9. Eisenstein and Kohn (eds.), *Mordecai M. Kaplan: An Evaluation* (New York: Reconstructionist Press, 1952), p. 116.
10. Mordecai Kaplan, *Judaism as a Civilization*, p. 550.

Decline of Civil Faith

When Rabbi Eisenstein wrote *Judaism under Freedom* in 1956, he could say, "No one would dare not rise for the national anthem."[11] After the traumas of Vietnam, the unresolved racial division, and Watergate, the sancta of civil religion have lost much of their prestige. As Sidney Ahlstrom said of the sixties, "The American moral and religious tradition was tested in this decade and found wanting."[12] Robert Bellah, the sociologist who first popularized the concept of civil religion, wrote in 1975, "Today the American civil religion is an empty and broken shell."[13]

It wasn't merely that American society failed, for a time, to live up to its ideals. Rather, the debunkers of history charged that the ideals themselves were at fault: the Vietnam War was not an aberration but an outgrowth of "Americanism." King's approach to civil rights, squarely within the best tradition of prophetic civil religion, was ultimately deemed ineffectual. Some historians argued that, in retrospect, this country had always been pluralistic only if one was willing to become a pseudo-WASP.[14] Will Herberg reminded us that becoming one of the establishment's "three American faiths" required of Judaism a sacrifice of prophetic distance; he had warned in the fifties that American religion was little more than a worship of the "American way of life."[15] Both among intellectuals and in the popular culture, there was a profound undermining of authority and respect for inherited institutions and American values. When protesters burned the American flag, they claimed it was out of love for country and a higher moral vision. Today, the specific issues are forgotten but the flag has not recovered. We have yet to recover the sacred reverence which our ancestors maintained toward their sancta. The Hebrew prophets, by contrast, railed against the misuse of the altar, but did not desecrate it.

Perhaps the loss of meaning and spiritual sustenance from the civil faith is what encouraged Americans to turn inward to their ethnic groups. This "new ethnicity," while a welcome force for many, has left our country sadly lacking an overarching structure to unify our common life. As

11. Ira Eisenstein, *Judaism under Freedom* (New York: Reconstructionist Press, 1956), p. 255.
12. Sidney Ahlstrom, *A Religious History of the American People* (New Haven: Yale University Press, 1972), p. 1085.
13. Robert Bellah, *The Broken Covenant* (New York: Seabury Press, 1975), p. 142.
14. John Murray Cuddihy, *No Offense: Civil Religion and Protestant Taste* (New York: Seabury Press, 1978).
15. Will Herberg, *Protestant-Catholic-Jew* (New York: Doubleday Press, 1955). See also Will Herberg, "America's Civil Religion: What It Is and Whence It Comes," in *American Civil Religion*, Richey and Jones, eds. (New York: Harper and Row, 1974), p. 87.

Barbara Hargrove noted, we have coasted along, assuming our pluralism was grounded in a single center of value.[16] We have found, however, in Yeats' famous words, "things fall apart; the centre cannot hold." The crisis in American civil faith may be based on valid moral insights or it may be an episode in American history in which we have temporarily lost our way. In either case, Reconstructionist thought, while not necessarily condoning the decline, must recognize it. If we do not, our theorizing will be increasingly irrelevant, based on an ideal America that does not exist.

For example, to base values education in public schools on the American civil faith now seems to base it on a weak foundation indeed. If underlying moral education is a vision of humanity and of the good life, what kind of vision underlies the secular "public school faith," and what are the sources of its authority? Jews hailed the Supreme Court decisions which banned sectarian influences from public schools, but with the civil faith in disrepute, we are left with a serious vacuum. We may find ourselves, as Queen Elizabeth II warned concerning England, "living on the moral capital which past generations have built up. Our children will suffer if we have no more to offer them than the virtues which we ourselves owe to an age of greater faith."[17]

Amidst the debris of public life, the Jewish traditionalists smile from their parochial schools and say "I told you so." In the wake of our disappointment, they urge us to do what they have done all along, to put our faith and energy into building a vital Judaism. In the end, the Jews have no one but the Jews. If we want to base our children's values in firm and fertile soil, then let us look to Judaism. There we have an ancient and rich tradition, still vibrant and worthy. The rest of the country will get along without us; it is time to take care of ourselves.

Decline of Jewish Life

As we turn inward in pursuit of our own meanings and concerns, we discover that the traditionalists' point is even stronger than we had thought. We prepare to tend our own garden only to discover that there is less of a garden left to tend. As the generations of immigrants die (a process which, excluding the wave of the 1940s, is reaching completion), we find ourselves increasingly dealing with "Jews in translation."[18]

---

16. Barbara Hargrove, "The Rise of a New Polytheism," *Religious Education* 72 (1977):459; and Barbara Hargrove, "Dilemmas of the New Spirtuality," *Religious Education* 73 (1978):259.
17. *Decision* (June, 1966), p. 1.
18. Phrase used by Frank Talmage, *Disputation and Dialogue* (New York: KTAV, 1975).

The Jews for whom Kaplan wrote in the thirties remembered an integral Jewish culture with a linguistic base. They were searching for an intelligent way to affirm something about their identities which they were not always happy about; they could not doubt, however, *that* they were Jews. They had been raised as Jews in ways they hardly knew, much as Molière's hero spoke prose all his life without being aware of it. Today, that set of memories and connections to Jewish life is vanishing. For our students, the "old neighborhood" is the suburbs.

With this acculturation of Jews to American society comes the recognition that we may need more than two or four hours a week to recreate Jewish culture. It is not entirely coincidental that when American Jews decided to "go ethnic" they found their most meaningful activities revolved around life in Israel. In the 1930s, Reconstructionism's insistence on a balance between Zion and Diaspora was important because of what it suggested for liberal Jews about Zion. Today, the position retains force, but the other side of the dialectic provides the needed corrective.

If we are to have an evolving Jewish civilization in the Diaspora, we must raise skilled, knowledgeable and committed Jews. The Sholom Aleichem of tomorrow is unlikely to emerge from a one-day-a-week Hebrew school. Socialization is a slow and intricate process. If, as Yeats says, "one can only reach out to the universe with a gloved hand," we are now discovering just how much effort it takes to clothe that hand with the glove of Judaism. We are learning that, Elie Wiesel notwithstanding, it is *not* enough to tell the story.

Synthesis

If we concede the erosion of American common faith and the need to look inward for spiritual and ethical sustenance as well as the full-time nature of the task of transmitting Jewish culture, we might conclude that parochial education, at least for some Jews, is the path for the future. Day schools in America are growing rapidly for many reasons: the ones outlined above are among the more admirable. Before Reconstructionists join the crowds rushing from the public schools, however, we need to recall the insights of the classical Reconstructionist position.

Can America really survive the fragmentation we are now witnessing, the loss of the social cement provided by the common faith? And if authentic America cannot survive, can Jews? Whatever the weaknesses of American civil faith, in practice or even in theory, Reconstructionism was basically right: a healthy America is healthy for Jews. Whether or not others now consider the reconstruction and realization of American ideals important, Jews cannot afford to give up on America. We may wish to turn inward and nurture our particularity for awhile, but if we abandon the polity and our democratic institutions fail us, no amount of day-schooling will save us. Similarly, the understandable desire to dodge inter-racial contact at a time of deteriorating relationships is ultimately an inadequate response. We must find ways to teach our culture, even if that means private education, without abandoning the public sector or the effort to purify and maintain a religion of democracy. The danger of parochial schools is that they create parochial people. We still live in two civilizations. Moreover, the American civilization still needs us.

The challenge is to transmit Jewish civilization intensively without simultaneously isolating students from the American society; its racial and religious pluralism, or its ideals and struggles. This would involve, perhaps, a unique kind of day school: a non-parochial parochial school, designed to prepare students to be contributing members of two civilizations. The following sketch presents a fantasy Reconstructionist Day School.[19] It is a fantasy which is realizable in certain cities in this country, given the requisite resources.

A Fantasy/Proposal

The setting is a large city with many ethnic groups, a large and varied Jewish community, and enormous social problems, among them inadequate public schools. The Reconstructionist Day School (hereafter referred to as RDS)[20] is located in the downtown area where many middle class Jews have recently resettled in close proximity to lower class communities. The school teaches all aspects of Jewish life and culture to children from every religious and secular movement within Judaism (this *is* a fantasy!).

The study of science, mathematics, and American history is carried on in conjunction with two neighboring schools: a Catholic parochial school and a Quaker day school, both of which are interracial. The students spend the afternoon at one of the three schools, depending on their grade, engaging in joint study as well as in gym and special programs. The celebration of American holidays is similarly planned and executed in conjunction with the other schools.

The formal curriculum of the American history course stresses the precarious and precious nature of democracy at the same time as it dis-

19. See also Benjamin and Judith Hollander, "Proposal for a Pluralistic Day School," *Reconstructionist* 36/3 (1970):23.
20. Reconstructionist in theory, but not in sole sponsorship. Ideally, the Jewish participation would cut across denominational lines. For a discussion of the dangers of day school education for intra-Jewish parochialism, see Jack J. Cohen, *Jewish Education in a Democratic Society* (New York: Reconstructionist Press, 1964), p. 312.

courages uncritical nationalism. The students learn and share with each other their respective group experiences in America. Supreme Court decisions and other historic documents are treated as the sacred texts of our country. The "hidden curriculum" of the joint courses is that students interact with each other and develop a group life as well as personal friendships.

Tzedakah is taught as a special unit in Jewish ethics each year. *Tzedakah* projects which the school sponsors are designed primarily to benefit the least well off in the nearby community, Jewish and non-Jewish. They are intended to prevent the choice of private education from becoming a choice to retreat from the problems of the city and society.

In addition to teaching the skills necessary for Jewish living, RDS emphasizes the civic skills of American life. These include an awareness of and interest in the political process. While the school does not endorse political candidates, it trains students in the work of political campaigning. The high school classes do not meet for several days prior to Election Day so that students can exercise their advocacy.

RDS provides the space in its facility for after-hours extracurricular activities which are open to the community. These include an extensive sports program, Boy Scouts, 4-H, a choir, and other activities engaged in by students of RDS as well as their age cohorts who live or go to school in the neighborhood. In this way, the students are encouraged to participate in the life of the community.

II. WHAT TO TEACH?

Classical Position

The Reconstructionist view of other faiths in this country, mainly Protestantism and Catholicism, is shaped by a context of healthy American pluralism. Kaplan's view of religious truth owes a great deal to the open society which formed and nurtured him. In a world in which another faith is not being forced upon one as the "only truth," it is possible to step back and see one's own faith as something other than the sole repository of revelation. Reconstructionism has argued that the other religions in this country represent other civilizations with their own equally valid attempts to concretize through sancta their values and their gropings toward an idea of God. Within the American scene, we have agreed amiably to look toward our own religious traditions while allowing maximal freedom for others to do the same. It is in such a context that it made sense to argue that the chosen people concept was inappropriate. In short,

Reconstructionism views other traditional American denominations as fellow participants in the American experiment in liberty.

The classical position seems to suggest that, to the extent Jewish education deals with other religions, it should do so without defensiveness or chauvinism. Other religions would be presented as other civilizations,[21] different from, but not better or worse than, Judaism.

That this view is radically at odds with that of traditional Judaism should be obvious. Less obvious is the departure from other forms of liberal Judaism. Because Reform saw Judaism as primarily, if not exclusively, a religion, it became necessary for it to show that this religion was in some way higher or better than other options.[22] Without such a polemical thrust, it would lose its *raison d'être*. Reconstructionism, on the other hand, requires no such claim in order to justify the continuation of Jews as Jews. Its argument is merely that Judaism is ours and it is right for us. Indeed, other civilizations often have insights which we lack and which we may freely borrow, expressing them in our own way through our own sancta.[23] Such an argument is perfectly suited to the theory behind American pluralism.

The "New Religions"

Beginning in the sixties, however, the religions around us have changed. We are no longer dealing, if we ever really were, with the tripartite faith world described by Will Herberg in *Protestant-Catholic-Jew*.[24] Perhaps to fill the void left by the decline of the civil faith, there have emerged on the religious scene new options which represent a challenge to Reconstructionist thinking. These groups are both a) unconcerned with liberal pluralism, and b) actively involved in proselytization. They offer spirituality, strong discipline, community, and a totalistic, exclusivistic vision.

The trend is visible everywhere. Among the Protestant denominations, the liberals are in decline and the conservative evangelical groups are growing.[25] In the Catholic world, charismatic options are on the rise,[26]

---

21. Kaplan, *Judaism as a Civilization*, p. 305.
22. See, for example, Leo Baeck, "Romantic Religion," in *Judaism and Christianity: Essays by Leo Baeck*, Walter Kaufmann, trans. (New York: Atheneum Press, 1970), p. 189.
23. Ira Eisenstein, "Equity in Inter-Faith Relations," *Reconstructionist* 7/12 (1941):6.
24. Ibid.
25. Dean Kelley, *Why Conservative Churches are Growing: A Study in Sociology of Religion* (New York: Harper and Row, 1972).
26. John Snook, *Going Further: Life and Death Religion in America* (Englewood Cliffs, N.J.: Prentice Hall, 1973), p. 127.

and the conservative forces in the Church are gaining ground. The growth of Hasidism reflects this movement, as do the more marginal groups such as Hare Krishna, Hebrew Christians, the Children of God, Dr. Moon's Unification Church, Meher Baba, and the Sufis.[27] These groups have become a matter of increasing concern to Jewish educators. They are not easily dealt with through Reconstructionist verities. We can no longer calmly say that the other religions are simply functions of other civilizations and should be respected as they respect us.

Whether or not Jews overestimate the threat to their ranks represented by missionaries—both Christian and cultic—the fact remains that American Jews perceive that the American tradition of tolerance is under attack. We see other Americans who no longer seem to be "playing by the rules," either of rational dialogue or of mutual non-interference. This calls into question for us the assumptions behind those rules. The American Jewish community has responded to the cults and Christian evangelism with understandable defensiveness, but also with a weakened devotion to religious liberty. Deprogramming cannot be the full answer; facing the larger issues posed by the cults is the more difficult long-term goal. On what basis does one deal with religions that do not share one's own commitment to religious tolerance? Eliezer Berkovits speaks for many confused and frightened parents when he says (and I do not quote out of context), "All we want of Christians is that they keep their hands off of us and our children."[28]

Kaplan did not envision, as he labored to make Judaism more acceptable (i.e., rational) for modern people, that it would be the irrational and spiritual dimensions of life that many post-moderns would seek in religion. Reconstructionism faces the challenge of making Judaism competitive on the open market to youth who find their other options to be very different in content and more aggressive in style. In the face of claims of superiority on the part of other groups, can we afford to continue our mild mannered, rational, and judicious approach to our religion and to others? Will we lose many who are looking for more complete answers or who long to say, with John Wesley, "I felt my heart strangely warmed"?[29]

The desire to combat missionary advances, particularly from Jewish Christians, has given rise to a plethora of courses for Jewish schools. For example, a non-copyrighted twenty-page document used by Hebrew schools in several parts of the country was written in response to the

---

27. Stoner and Parke, *All God's Children* (Radnor, Pa: Chilton Book Co., 1977).
28. Eliezer Berkovitz, "Judaism in the Post-Christian Era," *Judaism* 15 (1966):74.
29. *The Journal of John Wesley* (New York: Capricorn Books, 1963), p. 51.

Key '73 evangelical movement.[30] It provides an outline for a course in comparative religion entitled "Judaism and Christianity: Fundamental Differences." These differences include: Originality vs. Misappropriation, Freedom of Thought vs. Dogma, Monotheism vs. Polytheism, Law vs. Love, Justice and Mercy vs. Hypocrisy, Life vs. Death. For each of these dichotomies, the text claims that the first item of the pair is the Jewish way and is superior to the second, Christian approach.

This example may be a particularly vulnerable one, but it highlights the dangers to which such an approach is heir. Some of the contrasts reveal ignorance concerning Judaism, such as the notion that the Christian Scriptures misappropriate the Hebrew Bible but rabbinic Judaism does not. Others show naïveté concerning Christianity. For example, the meaning of the trinity—a doctrine that is in fact at odds with polytheism—is widely misunderstood by Jews. Still others, ironically, accept the dichotomies which Christianity perpetuated to undermine Judaism (law vs. love), merely reversing them and affirming the allegedly Jewish side. The irony is that some Christian scholars are now moving away from these dichotomies, finding them ethically malicious and historically inaccurate.[31]

Once comparative religion becomes an effort to show that our side is right and better, we inevitably confuse and obfuscate, distorting both our religion and the other, and creating faulty theological notions such as the idea that law and love are opposites. Finally, this business of mounting polemics against other faiths may blind us to an even more serious threat to Judaism—the secular faith options of the modern scene.

Secular Faith

A more crucial long term challenge to Judaism than the cults, although less recognized by the Jewish defense agencies, is the dominant American culture in which secularism has finally taken hold. The result has been a society whose values and world view is very different from that of Judaism. People still seek salvation, as they always have. In American life, however, that has now focused largely on the individual and his or her perfection. Our greatest fear might well be not that our children become Protestants, but that they truly become television-socialized Americans.

---

30. Phillip Brown, "Judaism and Christianity: Fundamental Differences," available from Phillip Brown, 1600 Niagra St., Denver, Colorado 80220.
31. See, for example, E. P. Sanders, *Paul and Palestinian Judaism* (Philadelphia: Fortress Press, 1977).

Philip Rieff called the dominant mid-twentieth century person "psychological man."[32] By this he meant an individual who no longer finds traditional religions meaningful, but who searches in psychology's techniques for personal salvation. Rieff's critique retains its force: "A sense of well-being has become the end rather than a byproduct of striving after some superior communal end."[33] In the early eighties, in the wake of est, best-seller self-help books, the religion of jogging, and varieties of "psychobabble," we may feel even more powerfully the corrective which Judaism offers to modern society. Only through grounding in an ancient and historically oriented civilization can an American today avoid the results of the mass culture's discontinuity with the past. This lack of connection with historically cherished values leaves us without important goals beyond our own improvement and makes us, finally, as Paul Goodman suggested, trivial.[34]

Franklin Littell has criticized the modern university for offering technology without values, for teaching in the same neutral way that the German universities did when training the core of professionals who later served the Nazi regime.[35] Yet students do not arrive at the modern university expecting to learn spiritual values; their expectations have been sufficiently reduced in public high schools. They expect to learn techniques. Virtue has become an intensely personal matter. This situation suggests that we revise our assumption that our chief competitors are other religions. Today, that is no longer the case.

Synthesis

Our updated Reconstructionist approach to other religions, then, must do battle simultaneously on two fronts. On the one hand, we want to demystify extremist religious options; on the other, we want to underscore the importance of religion, in light of the trivial self-oriented alternatives. We want to do this from within a Reconstructionist framework, without making claims for superiority, with which we disagree in principle. The belief that we do not possess the exclusive final word on God was *nurtured* by healthy pluralism but is not *philosophically dependent* upon

---

32. Philip Rieff, *The Triumph of the Therapeutic: Uses of Faith after Freud* (New York: Harper and Row, 1966).
33. R. D. Rosen, *Psychobabble* (New York: Avon Books, 1975), p. 18.
34. Paul Goodman, *New Reformation* (New York: Random House, 1970), p. 85.
35. Franklin Littell, "Die Glaubwurdigkeitskrise der modernen Universitat," unpublished address, June, 1979, available from Dr. Littell, Religion Department, Temple University, Philadelphia, Pennsylvania.

it. Indeed, we have a philosophical basis for our commitment to non-proselytizing which was carefully delineated by Rabbi Eisenstein in his doctoral dissertation.[36] Because Reconstructionism sees truths as universals and sancta as particulars, it is not necessary for an individual to switch groups when he recognizes truths in other religions. Rather, he can adapt the sancta he already possesses as a member of a historical community to better reflect his own needs and visions.

A Proposal

The following course is based on and attempts to illustrate the Reconstructionist approach to other religions outlined above. At the same time, it tries to be aware of the current situation and to make Judaism attractive and compelling in light of alternative options for spiritual or secular salvation.

This course approaches religions not in terms of their dogmas but in terms of one particular sanctum – the initiation rite. This is, according to Eliade, the most pervasive and perennial of all rituals.[37] Often erroneously referred to as a puberty rite, this ritual of admission to adult society takes place between the ages of ten and twenty, depending upon the culture. Initiation rites are also performed when an individual of any age enters the group as a convert. This latter use is a special case of what is normally the culture's way of celebrating and "cushioning" the "life cycle crisis" of the adolescent. Since the course was designed for students between the ages of thirteen and sixteen (the time when they are first and perhaps best able to view religion comparatively),[38] this rite was selected to serve as a window into the function of religion. The reason should be obvious: the transition involved is one of compelling interest to the students. At the same time, it has the advantage of allowing a treatment of both cults and secular culture within a larger context.

Van Gennep noted that, in primitive cultures, life cycle changes are perceived as times of danger, upsetting to the individual and to the community.[39] The rite is a way of dealing with this disturbance in a formal setting that acknowledges the fear but transcends it by reaffirming the

---

36. Ira Eisenstein, *The Ethics of Tolerance Applied to Religious Groups in America* (New York: Crown Press, 1941).

37. Quoted in Harvey Cox, *The Seduction of the Spirit* (New York: Simon and Schuster, 1973), p. 43.

38. Inhelder and Piaget, *The Growth of Logical Thinking from Childhood to Adolescence* (New York: Basic Books, 1958).

39. Arnold van Gennep, *The Rites of Passage* (London: Routledge and Kegan Paul, 1960).

community and its values. Reading van Gennep in conjunction with Erikson,[40] it becomes clear that the trauma involved in each life cycle crisis is at base a religious one: how will meaning be renegotiated at the new stage of development?

Course Objectives

1) To introduce students to a Reconstructionist way of viewing religious phenomena, not as divinely revealed commands, but as human creations meeting human needs.
2) To discuss the fears and challenges of adolescence (sexuality, career choice, acceptance by the group, identity formation) and show how different rites succeed or fail in addressing these issues.
3) To encourage respect for the seriousness and importance of religious issues and religious sancta.
4) To show students how cultural values (physical courage, intellect, material success, fertility) are translated into ritual, and to encourage them to be aware of Jewish values and of their own.
5) To underscore the commonality of human experiences despite differences in specifics.
6) To help students better understand the American culture in which they live and to encourage them in a subtle way to see their Jewish civilizational involvement as filling serious lacunae in that culture.
7) To demystify the missionary religion or cult by encouraging students to take a humanistic, cross-cultural perspective. This view of religion is perhaps the best "barrier," as Henry Shreibman put it, to the fundamentalism of the proselytizing group.[41]
8) To offer a practical experience in remaining Jewish in the face of a wide variety of options. Each of these rites may have aspects that appeal to us or express values we find attractive. Only the Jewish rite is our own.[42] That means that it is ours to change as well as to preserve. To the extent that the Jewish rite does not meet all our needs, it is our responsibility to practice "creative Judaism." It is the actual laboratory practice of this activity which is the climax of the course.

---

40. Erik Erikson, *Identity, Youth and Crisis* (London: Faber and Faber, 1968).
41. Henry Shreibman, *The Cult Phenomenon*, Baltimore Board of Jewish Education, in cooperation with the American Association for Jewish Education, 1978.
42. Eisenstein, 1941, *The Ethics of Tolerance*.

Course Sessions[43]

1) Kikuyus of Kenya. The public circumcision of an adolescent boy.
2) Sioux Indians. A youth goes to a mountaintop for several days alone to "cry for a vision."
3) American Baptist. A teenager is baptized in church in what Harvey Cox calls "a real trip."
4) Navajo Indian. A girl at the onset of menstruation engages in a number of private and public ceremonies.
5) Jewish bar/bat mitzvah. How well did your bar/bat mitzvah function for you?
6) Secular America. What is the initiation rite? Passing the driving test? Voting for the first time? High school prom? The first drug trip? Why does American society not have a uniform rite? Is this good or bad? What happens to people without religions in such a context?
7) Initiation rite of a cult popular in the community (Unification Church, Hare Krishna, etc.). What needs does this rite fill? What values does it express?
8) Designing and performing the students' own creative Jewish initiation rite, meeting the needs of adolescence and expressing Jewish values as the students choose to understand these. Several small groups of students each create their own rite and perform it for the class using one of the students as the "initiating" youth.

Conclusion

The groundwork for thinking first laid by the great Reconstructionists decades ago has not disappointed us. Despite important changes in the current scene, the theories remain sound and, if anything, in greater need of being heard. Our attempts to create schools and programs that apply these insights to our own situation is what constitutes the excitement of being a Reconstructionist educator in the last decades of the twentieth century. The above ideas are experimental models. The task before us remains: How can they, or other plans seeking to address the same problems, meet the challenge?

---

43. Course materials are available from Nancy Fuchs-Kreimer, Reconstructionist Rabbinical College.

Integrating Jewish and Secular Studies in the Jewish Day School

■ ■ ■ Sara Caine and Paula Halfon

The American Jewish child is exposed to many intellectual and cultural experiences. In a human way, the integration of these varied and fragmented experiences is a lifelong struggle. The identity of a Jewish child is shaped by two distinct streams of experience—one Jewish, one American—and this presents both unique opportunities and problems.

The American Jewish child naturally will develop different strategies for coping with his/her dual identity. One of the alternatives available to that child is to isolate him/herself as a Jew, thereby depriving him/herself of participation in the rich and varied cultural diversity of our pluralistic society. On the other hand, if the uniqueness of a Jewish identity poses problems for the child, s/he may choose to assimilate and repress his/her Jewish identity. S/he may even choose to negate it.

Ideally, the (non-Orthodox) day school, as a model institution, seeks to give the child a holistic environment in which s/he can confront and explore, in a supportive atmosphere, his/her own experiences as an American Jew. In such an atmosphere, the child may raise questions freely regarding perceptions of his/her own identity, both in relation to other Jews and in connection with the non-Jewish community. The implicit goal is to facilitate the development of a positive self-image, which reflects the process of integrating the many aspects of the child as both American and Jew.

Each of us has participated in varied educational settings, as both teachers and students. It has been our observation that, in many cases, when a child enters a Jewish school, s/he is confronted with a segregated, departmentalized organization with separate curricula, separate teachers, and separate responsibilities. This type of framework, whether in a self-contained day school or in the combination of a public school/supplemental school setting, does not help to facilitate the integration process.

Recognizing this problem and sharing the desire to encourage the development of the "whole" child, we have taken advantage of our sixth grade Solomon Schechter Day School environment to develop a curriculum which integrates secular and Jewish studies. Our answer to this paramount educational problem is an interdisciplinary approach to the stated curriculum.

An interdisciplinary approach in education is not a new concept. Many progressive public school teachers expand their otherwise narrow foci to include other curricular areas. A prime example of this concept is Jerome Bruner's *Man: A Course of Study* (Boston: Educational Development Center, 1969-72), where social studies are expanded to include language arts and science among other otherwise isolated curricular areas.

Many in the field of Jewish education have also discovered this concept. Curriculum designs are available which present Jewish history against the backdrop of the general history of the time (e.g., the Menorah Curriculum, United Synagogue of America, 1977). Our approach attempts to take this concept one step further by bringing together general and Jewish studies in shared activities and experiences.

Our bilingual, bicultural curriculum design, which is classroom tested, actually integrates concepts and themes in the children's secular and Jewish studies. The lessons are designed according to the following sequence: 1) an examination, in depth, of separate parallel cultures; 2) comparing and contrasting themes, issues, and historical events through team teaching; and 3) an active integration of the bicultural dimensions, to explore their interrelationships and interdependence, and to anticipate their applications for the future.

We developed our units around the theme "Myth, Midrash and Legend." The framework of integrating the study of myths and legends from many cultures provided us with the flexibility to challenge the children's thought processes in a unique way. The children became active participants in their own education. They themselves were the explorers. Not only did they "discover" the knowledge, but they also reached the conclusions and identified the implications. This method requires, as it develops, a sharpening of the children's critical thinking. It also demands that the students continually evaluate and assess their discoveries as they accumulate them throughout the year.

What follows is a brief overview of a successfully executed unit—our introductory unit on "Religion in Society." We began with the concurrent examination of creation stories. In Jewish studies, the students critically examined the first chapter of Genesis, as well as selections from *Hebrew Myths*, by Robert Graves and Raphael Patai (New York: Greenwich House, Crown Publishers, 1983). The students demonstrated a sophisticated understanding in their identification of certain surprising elements in the literature. For example, they posed questions concerning the placement of primeval monsters in the chronology of creation.

Concurrently, in general studies, the students studied creation myths from American Indian tribes, Japan, China, and Mexico, taken from Mircea Eliade's *Gods, Goddesses and Myths of Creation* (Harper and Row, 1967). In their evaluation, the students found discrepancies in the sequence of creation and posed similar questions for each of these stories. They began to discover, assess, and tabulate common denominators.

Frustrated in their need for answers, they themselves initiated the second step in the process. We were bombarded with questions, both in the classroom and out on the playground, seeking to fill the gaps. The students had begun to struggle with their own questions: In what ways is the Torah different from these myths? Can we believe in and study science without contradicting our trust in Torah? It was at this point that we shared their need to integrate the two disciplines and reach some conclusions as a class.

The second step involved team-taught lessons in which teachers facilitated the comparison of the non-Jewish myths with Genesis 1. We charted the myths according to common and disparate elements. These elements included both time and sequence of creation. Our immediate conclusion, at the end of this lesson, was a unanimous agreement that each creation myth is a culturally appropriate metaphor which answered the needs and questions of the people of the time. The myths provided a structure through which ancient people could understand the world. As modern thinkers, we can still view the world through the poetry of Torah for the values it expresses.

Having arrived at an understanding of the diachronic significance of the creation story, the children were still not satisfied with the role of evolution in the creation process. They still needed to know how creation and evolution could be accepted side by side without contradiction.

We remained concerned that the children discover the answers to these questions themselves. To bring this unit to a culmination the children viewed the film *Inherit the Wind*, which illustrates the power of "belief" and its effect on social norms. In a follow-up discussion, they compared issues raised by them in class with those raised in the film. Among the issues were: freedom of speech, the right of free access to information, and the right to personal belief without legislative interference.

Happily, they empathized with the problems in the courtroom, and were convinced that these questions are still encountered in the classroom. We provided the environment that could help them make the transition from comparing motifs of creation stories to bringing the values in the creation stories into a contemporary perspective. Along with a debate on evolution versus creation, they explored the further implications of separation of church and state. As they are day school students, this is an issue which touches them personally.

This introductory unit gave the children a foundation on which to approach subsequent units. As part of a general unit on Sumer/Babylonia, the children examined the Gilgamesh flood story. Concurrently, in Jewish studies, the children studied the biblical account of Noah and the Flood. This unit was highlighted in the comparison and contrast of the stories, and in the cultural metaphors they reflected. Months later, when studying Greece, it was evident that the students had held on to concepts they had discovered in this comparison. In a lesson designed to focus on Greek mythology, one child presented a book she had borrowed from the library, that included the Greek accounts of creation and of a flood story. The rest of the class rallied to her cause in demanding to examine yet another culture's rendition of an already familiar topic.

In a later lesson on Moses as a leader, the children drew comparisons between Moses – a radical, a seeker of justice, and a man with a dream – and modern leaders with the same characteristics. Some other units which the children explored within this curricular framework have included energy and *Tu B'Shevat*, comparative governmental systems and oppressed peoples, and ancient Egyptian society.

These descriptions hardly do justice to the actual excitement with which our students approached these units. The framework we have developed represents not only a method of thinking in the sixth grade classroom, but also one which can be applied to other classroom environments and grade levels. Our success indicates that we have begun to pave the first precious steps of what promises to be a long and sweet journey. Our children have assimilated wisdom which has helped to shape their identity as participants in the Jewish, American, and world communities. This definition of learning in a bilingual, bicultural day school facilitates the growth of a knowledgeable, well-rounded child in whom we might place our hope for the future.

Family Days and
Family Education

■ ■ ■ Beth Kellman

Morning rituals become ingrained in the daily lives of families. Sunday morning, in particular, has become a time when parents of children in religious schools wake up abruptly to the sound of an early morning alarm. Up and out the door with bagel in hand. The Sunday morning car pool begins. At school there are calls of "See you in two hours" from parents to their children who are walking slowly inside.

The responsibility for the continuation of this ritual rests with two parties: parents and religious schools. Parents have relied upon the one- or two-day-a-week religious school to "make" their children Jews in sixty-four hours per year. The religious school has confirmed this view by shutting its doors and establishing "walls" between the parking lot and the classroom. It appears that educators have been afraid to share what goes on inside the classroom. It is the thesis of this article that it is time to share our curricula, open our doors to parental involvement, and provide teacher training for family education.

Education, in fact, should begin at home and be continued in greater depth at religious school. But the tradition of transmitting Jewish life and culture through the home is disappearing. The Jewish community is assimilating and priorities are shifting. Blaming the home for the failure of our religious education can no longer be an acceptable response. We must encourage families to reaffirm their responsibility for Jewish education in the home in conjunction with education at school. It is important that educators and families begin to share in the religious education process. The student and the family unit must become the means of transmitting the essence and meaning of Jewish life. This approach can best be achieved by including the family in active learning programs at school.

Participatory experience, rather than exclusive use of conventional book learning, will alter the perspective of those parents who often say to their children: "I hated Sunday School, so therefore you may, too—just accept it." This change in focus and format may bring a new comment: "Our Sunday School wasn't like this. I'm glad as an adult I can share this with you."

Of course, working with the Jewish family means working with the changed societal realities which have affected Jewish and non-Jewish families alike. We must examine these families, who are the participants in our programs. Over fifty years ago, Dr. Mordecai Kaplan wrote the following in *Judaism as a Civilization* (p. 416f.):

> Since Judaism is more than a religion or a religious philosophy, it cannot even begin to function in the individual as such. The family is the smallest social unit through which it can articulate itself....The minimum unit of a civilization consists of man, wife and child, for no person by himself can be the carrier of a civilization, which depends upon the social interaction as well as upon transmission of cultural content from one generation to the next....It is necessary, therefore, to consider the readjustment which the home must undergo in order that it may continue to influence Jewish civilization, and to be influenced by it.

Though Kaplan's definition may have applied to the American Jewish community of his era, changes in family structure make the involvement he proposes even more necessary. Today we must be willing to accept a change in definition of Kaplan's "minimum unit" if we are to be sensitive to the needs of Jewish civilization. Alternative family units exist and must be included; e.g., single parents with children, divorced families with split visitation, one Jewish parent with children, and homosexual families with children. These family units, in particular, often rely on and seek out the Jewish community to create a larger familial experience, often taken for granted by Kaplan's "minimum unit." Our schools can play an integral role in the transmission of our civilization if all are included, conventional and unconventional.

The curricula of family education will vary from community to community, according to the community's ideology and affiliation, but the process and goals should remain constant. Educators need to generate support for the school as well as interest in the school. Curricula, long and short, which are sent home at the beginning of the year are not enough to encourage active support. Open house meetings which are held at school once a year do not institute an open line of communication between parent and teacher. These meetings, though important, do not allow parents to participate in the learning process. If families are invited to experience the educational process in ongoing activities, the rewards are enhanced for both parties.

Encouraging Family Participation

One of the most successful methods which serves to include this kind of rewarding experience is the institution of family days. Family days are those days or events set aside in the calendar when families come to the school together to participate in a specific program.

Materials explaining the goals of family days can be designed and sent home at the beginning of the year. If it is the educator's expectation that parents will have an active role in these days, that should be explained. Given the choice between returning to sleep on Sunday and participating in a meaningful program, many parents may choose the excitement of a learning experience.

The publicity regarding these days is very important. Families should be mailed reminders as the date for a family day approaches. If possible, preparatory materials such as articles and a bibliography can be sent home. Many people feel more comfortable if they are familiar with the theme of the day and can come with some knowledge of the material to be covered. In order to initiate a positive response, it is helpful to promote a sense of responsibility for the day. Families may be requested to bring a family story, food to share, or materials needed for a project. This may reassure them that their physical presence will become a necessary part of the program.

Telephone chains are very helpful in coordinating the day. Room parents or other volunteers may make a personal phone call encouraging participation. We want families to come to school feeling as much a part of the community as possible. If a parent is telephoned and responds that he or she cannot attend, he or she should be encouraged to send the child anyway. When everyone arrives, the teacher may request that parents include these students in their family unit.

Educators and Staff: Sharing Responsibility

It is often helpful to arrange a workshop which enables the staff to focus upon the specific teaching skills which are needed to work with a mixed-aged group. Various pedagogic techniques can be explored. As the particular family day approaches, the staff can meet and begin to apply the techniques to the particular theme which is being developed. Background material about the theme of the family day can be distributed.

It is important that this material be used on many levels. The educator may suggest participatory activities. The following techniques often are successful: the use of a Seder format (based on the Passover Seder and adapted to other holiday celebrations), drama (families prepare skits to perform for class), creative writing projects, fairs or carnivals that can be actual reenactments of a time period (Lower East Side fair, shtetl day, Israel fair), studying primary source material, map making, and time lines. These techniques avoid lecturing, which often means talking to one age group and losing the other. It is important to remind teachers not to depend on the parents to teach a subject to their children. We must assume that everyone comes to learn on family days.

It is important that teachers be briefed on the community with which they will deal. The educator's experience in working with the community should be shared with the staff. Parents with teaching experience and/or active members of the synagogue may be pointed out to teachers as "aides." If a teacher desires help from the parents in presenting basic material, you might suggest they send the material home to allow parents the opportunity to prepare.

The staff should be given the chance to voice their fears and discomforts as well as their excitement with the idea of parents coming to school. The staff workshop should be held several weeks in advance. The educator may want to meet individually with teachers to discuss their plans for the day. It is essential that the staff be well prepared for the day.

Successful Techniques

The teacher can employ several pedagogic techniques for working with large groups. The teacher may break the large group into small groups of families and ask them to study some material. These smaller groups provide a more intimate atmosphere and allow for more communication between participants. The material may be available for them to use in the class, or they may be instructed to go to the library. This often gives parents their first opportunity to view and use the library.

It is also possible to separate children and adults during the day. Ask the rabbi or another educator to give a "How to..." workshop with the parents while the students prepare for another part of the day. Material can be distributed to go home with the families such as songs, background material, additional reference material, or suggested stories and field trips.

Creating a spirit and enthusiasm for the day is an important part of a successful program. Think about your participants. Often students in grades six through nine are reluctant to participate in programs with their parents. These students can be given special responsibilities which allow them to feel needed and special. Perhaps they can direct people upon arrival, distribute food and materials, or assist teachers of younger grades. Let them know you have expectations regarding their participation. That extra encouragement can be the incentive you seek to stimulate their attendance. This sense of being relied upon often takes the pressure off those parents who want their children to attend but do not want to force them to do so.

It is important that the day be well organized and run as smoothly as possible. Make schedules available to parents. Label classrooms, teachers, and grades on the door of each classroom.

You may want to prepare a list of administrative details. Here are several questions you might ask yourself in preparing your own list:

> How long will the day be?
> Will you provide a meal or any refreshments?
> Who will distribute the food?
> Where will the program be held?
> Will you include the entire school?
> What is the role of the teacher? the student? the parent? the educator?
> What is the role of the family?
> Will the families be asked to prepare something in advance?
> Do you need to hire specialists? A day-care worker for families who want to bring younger children?
> What materials can be sent home in advance?
> Will phone calls be made to ask people to attend?
> What special responsibilities will be given to students?
> What are the goals for the day?
> How does the program fit into the entire year's curriculum?

Sample Family Day: Sukkot

What follows is a description of a Sukkot Family Day that took place at Congregation Rodef Sholom in San Rafael, California. Each family was contacted through the mail and by telephone. Every student was encouraged to ask his or her parents to come. Families were asked, by phone, to bring something to eat (fruit, vegetables, or juice, to be selected from one of four colors ranging from light to dark) and a blanket to sit on. Families with more than one child were asked to choose one of their children's grades to go to as a family. Families with more than one adult often opted to split up. The decision was left up to each family.

Students worked with their teachers beforehand, preparing material for a Sukkot Seder. The Seder was to be the central theme and technique of the Family Day. Student participation in the writing of the Sedarim was crucial to the success of the day. This was apparent to the students, and they were motivated by the sense of responsibility.

The families arrived at school carrying fruits, vegetables, and juices. The atmosphere in the halls was noticeably different from a regular Sunday. Families were walking and talking together. There was a feeling of excitement and celebration everywhere. There were signs and fliers available at several places outlining the schedule for the day.

During the first forty minutes, the adults were given a choice between attending a workshop conducted by the rabbi or going to class with their children. In the workshop, entitled "How to Celebrate Sukkot at Home," the rabbi discussed the history of the holiday and instructed and encouraged families to build their own sukkot.

In class, the students and parents made decorations for the synagogue sukkah, or prepared for their Sukkot Seder (held later that day). As the families worked, they were given the opportunity to explore their child's classroom. The students' textbooks and workbooks were available for browsing. There were folders with completed work by each student. This gave parents a chance to see the Sunday morning environment of their children, and it brought the classroom experience closer to their lives.

One class at a time came down with their parents to decorate the synagogue sukkah. The parents were especially helpful with the younger children, because they could lift children up to decorate. Among the decorations were paper chains, crayon rubbings of leaves, and flower bouquets (picked by the families on a walk), dove mobiles, and an *Ushpizin* (guests) mural. (*Ushpizin* is the custom of inviting our ancestors to join us in the sukkah. Our older students invited contemporary figures and created a mural depicting them.)

After the sukkah was decorated and the adult workshop was completed, each class assembled for the Sukkot Seder. To prepare teachers to write a Seder, copies of the *Sukkot Seder* by Cherie Koller-Fox and another by Howard Wasserman were distributed, as well as one prepared for reference use that was filled with stories and background material. Many classes chose to celebrate outside. The Seder format allowed learning to take place without assuming previous knowledge. Questions were asked and answered. Stories were shared and songs were sung. Everyone had a chance to teach each other. The grounds of the school came alive in a special way because of the inclusion of families.

The class Seders lasted approximately forty-five minutes. The staff music and dance specialists circulated and were asked to take an active role in the Sedarim. Several older students were given the responsibility of taking a *lulav* and *etrog* around to each Seder and explaining their significance. Every family was given a copy of the class Seder to bring home. At the culmination of the day, everyone gathered in a central area for a story told by the rabbi, followed by group singing and dancing. There was a short Kiddush in the newly decorated sukkah so that everyone could see the work of our families.

People left that day happy to have experienced a learning situation. Parents were more supportive as the year continued because of their direct experience in the classroom. In many cases, they were more familiar with the teachers and felt comfortable with subsequent communication. Because Sukkot falls at the beginning of the school calendar, parents felt that they were a part of the school from the beginning of the year. The excitement from this day was relayed to those who did not participate, thereby creating anticipation for the next Family Day.

Sample Family Day: Hanukah

The theme for this day was related to our year-long school unit on *tzedakah*. It was titled Community *Tzedakah* Day. The goal was to teach the meaning of giving through actions. We wanted our students to learn that it is not enough to collect change each week. Our working assumption was that students must actively participate in giving something of themselves if the true meaning of *tzedakah* is to be taught and understood. It was decided that families would move from classroom to classroom, making tangible items to be given away as gifts for Hanukah. It was also decided that the songs and blessings of Hanukah would be taught.

In preparation, teachers were asked to choose with their class an agency or other recipient of their Family *Tzedakah* Project. Once the class decided, they spent several sessions learning about the agency. Some classes invited a guest to come to discuss the work of the agency chosen. Classrooms were decorated with pictures, stories, and posters to illustrate the agency which the class had chosen to receive its *tzedakah*.

A faculty meeting was held so that teachers could share the decisions which classes had made about recipient agencies. Activities were discussed which would underscore the themes of Hanukah and *tzedakah*. The guidelines were: (1) something that could be made and could be given; (2) something with a connection to Hanukah; (3) something that actively taught the meaning of *tzedakah*; and (4) something that would enable families to work together. The following projects were decided upon:

Grade	Recipient	Project	Objective
K	Soviet Jewry	Hanukah cards to Jews in Russia	Create an awareness of the plight of Jews in the Soviet Union
1	Local Jewish hospital (Pediatrics)	Hanukah storybooks	Learn the story of Hanukah
2	Alyn Hospital (Jerusalem)	Pen Pal project started with patients	Initiate friendship with Jewish children in Israel
3	Ourselves	Construction of Maimonides' Ladder of Tzedakah	Teach the value of *tzedakah* through figures in Jewish history
4	Jewish Braille Institute	Make tapes of Hanukah blessings and songs for Jewish blind	Teach and review blessings; help those who are blind
5	Synagogue library	Posters encouraging donation of books for Hanukah and life-cycle events	Exposure to library; teach that gifts can be given to library
6	Jewish home for seniors	Make *Hanukiot* for the Home	Make something to give away; creating your own *Hanukiah*
7	Ourselves	Acting out skits written by seventh graders about the history and services of the Jewish Family Service	Learn of ways in which Jewish agencies help people

A list of the projects was mailed to the parents in a letter describing the Hanukah Family Day with background material about Hanukah, *tzedakah*, and a bibliography of books about Hanukah.

The day of celebration arrived. Families were assembled in groups of twenty participants as they entered the school. They were given a packet containing Hanukah material to be taken home as well as a schedule for the day. Directions were enclosed which instructed them about which rooms they were to go to, and at what time. Because groups were sent off as soon as they arrived, people were not kept waiting. Those who arrived late had fewer projects in which they could participate. There were four projects that could be completed by each group if they arrived on time. The teacher of each grade remained in his or her classroom. The groups did the moving. This was especially good for the younger members of a family, as their attention spans are limited. Each project took about twenty minutes. All the materials needed for the projects were in the classrooms.

At the end of the day everyone assembled for singing, dancing, eating *sufganiot* (jelly donuts, an Israeli custom) and for the sharing of our projects. The concept of helping others and sharing our knowledge touched the lives of every participant.

In most cases, it was the responsibility of the educator to distribute the completed projects. The seventh graders decided to take *Hanukiot* to the home for seniors and present a short Hanukah program. Many of the parents attended as well.

The school received many letters of thanks from various organizations. They were displayed on a bulletin board for all to read. The sixth graders prepared the bulletin board. The spirit of this day was kept alive for many weeks.

Evaluating Family Programs

There is always room for improvement, even in the best family program. Soliciting responses from those who participated is of the utmost importance. It gives the participants the feeling that their opinion matters. Often negative criticism is the only feedback that comes to the attention of the educator. How often are positive comments shared? Creating a format of evaluation insures that both negative and positive responses can be shared, and may prove to be invaluable to the educator. Educators should be visible during the Family Day to talk with parents and students. This also gives the educator firsthand knowledge of the Family Day. But visibility is not a sufficient tool for evaluation. Written responses give the participant a chance to reflect on the day as well as to present tangible feedback for the educator. Photographs also act as reminders of the day's events, and often capture expressions that are not apparent through the written word.

A questionnaire to be completed at the end of the day is the most expedient way of compiling feedback. This eliminates waiting to have them returned to the office several days later. The experience of the day is still fresh in the participants' minds. In the evaluation, the educator wants to be able to capture both elation and disappointment. A bibliography of reference material relating to the Family Day might be attached to the evaluation form.

The following are sample questions that might be incorporated into an evaluation:

When and how did you learn about the Family Day?
How many members of your family participated? What ages?
What workshops did you attend?
Were you able to meet your child(ren)'s teacher(s)?
Was it possible to view his or her completed work?
Did you meet new families? Did your child(ren) know his or her classmates?
Was there enough time for you in each workshop?
What new things did your family learn?
Did you receive new material to bring home?
Would you be interested in a follow-up day?
What did your family enjoy most about the day? Please be specific.
What did your family enjoy least?
Which of your questions were left unanswered?
Do you have suggestions for other Family Days?
Do you have suggestions for how we could have improved upon this program?

It is wise to share the results of the evaluation with the staff. Given that the project has been a collective staff effort, all the participants should experience both the praise and the criticism.

The teachers should be instructed to conduct a follow-up lesson the next time the class meets. We must remember to give added support to those who participated. Family Days are not to be considered vacation days from Sunday School, but as part of the curriculum. On the other hand, those who did not attend should not be penalized. Negative actions often receive attention in class. It is imperative that we recognize those students who came and that we have the teachers ask them for verbal feedback: Which projects did you complete? Did you teach your parents something new? Did they teach you something new? Perhaps a tutoring arrangement can be instituted for those who were absent. This will enhance the feeling of importance and self-esteem for those who came, while allowing those who did not come a chance to see that they did, in fact, miss something.

The best way to capture the true feeling of the day is to have someone take photographs. Display the photographs on the bulletin board. This reminds the student of the day and can be used as publicity for subsequent Family Days.

As educators, we must evaluate our programs continually. Integrating Family Days into our school curricula will encourage and strengthen religious education, insuring that it will continue into the home. The integration of religious school education and the home experience is the key to successful transmission of Jewish life for the participants.

Through the experiences created on Family Days such as those described above, it is hoped that parents will become more interested in the education of their children both in the school and at home. By altering our educational techniques in these ways, we can begin to hope that our schools will grow in size and in spirit. If we can create programs which are successful in strengthening the Jewish activity of family units, our students will have an ever-broadening sense of their Jewish identity.

The Seder Shel Shabbat

■ ■ ■ A Brief Introduction

Beginning with Kaplan's earliest writings, one of the distinguishing characteristics of Reconstructionism has been its emphasis on the development of programs which move Jewish life out of the synagogue and back into the home. These programs respond to the needs of informed, educated lay people who, rejecting the binding nature of the halakhah and hence the model of the rabbi as halakhic authority, want to struggle with and practice the tradition unassisted. Thus, Jewish sancta could be experienced in ways that were emotionally satisfying and conducive to personal and familial growth.

A concrete example of this Reconstructionist approach is the Seder Shel Shabbat. Kaplan's formal proposal for the institution of the Friday evening home seder was published in 1972 and is reprinted here. The idea, however, is inherent in his earliest writings. (See, for example, *Judaism as a Civilization*, 1967 edition, pp. 443-447.)

Following this proposal, Reconstructionist educators have developed Shabbat Seder programs for synagogue schools as a way of introducing students *and their families* to the spirit of Shabbat, so that the experience could then be recreated by those families in their homes. Such a program was developed in 1973 at the Ann Spak Thal School of Society Hill Synagogue in Philadelphia by Joel and Rebecca Alpert. Joel Alpert describes the program in the essay which follows Kaplan's.

The Sabbath Eve Seder:
An Indispensable Innovation*

■ ■ ■ Mordecai M. Kaplan

The Jews of the world today, except for anti-Semitic purposes, constitute an anonymous amalgam of human beings with no functioning bond
of unity. The most serious symptom of this abnormal situation is the
uncertainty with regard to Jewish identity. This has recently been demonstrated on two occasions: one in Israel, where Ben-Gurion's appeal to
about two hundred Jewish scholars for an answer to the question "Who
is a Jew?" proved to be in vain; the other in America, where an anthro-
pologist, in an article on the subject of Jewish identity, wrote: "No word
means more things to more people than the word Jew." That means that
Jews nowadays lack that group consciousness which throughout the past
united all Jews throughout the world with a sense of mutual responsibility, and which was a source of happiness to every Jew individually.
Both in order for them to regain that happiness, and to recover the history-
making ability of their group consciousness, Jews have to be formally and
publicly reconstituted as a people. That is the only way it can be saved
from the fate that overcame the Lost Ten Tribes of Israel.

A History-Making People

However, are the Jews fully aware of the danger to their survival as a
people? The answer is certainly in the negative. Those who are concerned
look to Zionism as the solution. The marginal Jews, whose number is

* Reprinted from *Reconstructionist* 38/2 (1972):17-20.

legion, are not at all concerned. As for the rest, who amount to about half the number of Jews, something has to be done to reawaken in them enough of a desire to prevent the Jewish people from becoming absorbed by the various populations among which it is dispersed to demand that they be formally and publicly reconstituted as a people *de jure*. For that to be the case, a way has to be found whereby that "saving remnant" might become aware of the history-making genius of the Jewish people throughout its entire past of about thirty-five centuries.

To be a history-making people means to contribute to the enhancement of human life and the creative fulfillment of its most worthwhile potentialities. For that it is not enough to produce writers of history. It means being collectively as a people so aware of its history as to derive from it a sense of destiny which is that of being a source of blessing to all other peoples and nations in the world. To recover that history-making ability as a people, Jews have to get to know the past of their people, with its promise for their own future as well as for that of the rest of the world. To that end it is of utmost importance to introduce into Jewish life an innovation of an educative character, the practice every Friday night of the Sabbath Eve Seder, analogous in spirit and purpose to the Pesah Eve Seder.

One Seder a Year Not Enough

Why the Pesah Seder as a model? Because its purpose is to educate the Jewish people in the art of functioning as a history-making people. That is the art of transmitting the social and spiritual heritage from one generation to the next. To succeed in that art, the education has to be adapted to the character and maturity of each child. Thus, the four-fold repetition of the command in the Torah for parents to acquaint their children with the story of the Exodus from Egypt, which marks the beginning of the history-making career of the Jewish people, is interpreted as referring to four different types of children: the wise child, the stubborn child, the naive child, and the very young child who has to be taught to ask questions.

In view of the present critical situation of the Jewish people, one such Seder a year, no matter how well conducted, even with the aid of the *New Haggadah*, is far from enough. Every Friday night must be used to conduct a Sabbath Eve Seder for the transmission of the Jewish heritage from parents to children; this has become indispensable to the parents as well as to the children. However, instead of a fixed liturgical text, as the Pesah Seder, the Sabbath Eve Seder has to include first the consecutive reading each Friday night of selections from some major standard work which might serve as the basic text for at least two years. By that time, we may assume, the family will be prepared to make use of other sources of their choosing. If enough families take this innovation seriously, sufficient interest would be aroused in the Jewish history and destiny as to expedite the formal and public reconstitution of the Jewish people.

Friday Night Home Night

Apart from the foregoing direct purpose to be served by the Sabbath Eve Seder, the following spiritual purposes might also be achieved:

In the first place, it would reinstate the one religious institution which has done more than any other to render the functioning of religion the most humanizing aspect of a people's life style or civilization. No less a modernist Jewish thinker than Ahad Ha-am has written: "There is more significance to the observance of the Sabbath than the fact that the Jewish people kept it; it is the fact that the Sabbath observance kept the Jewish people alive."

In *Judaism as a Civilization* (1934) there is the following passage concerning the Sabbath: "In the last instance it is not what the Jew will refrain from doing on the Sabbath, but the affirmative conduct which the observance of the Sabbath will elicit from him. The Sabbath must make itself felt in the home. Only there can its observance be made attractive enough to impel the Jew to effort and sacrifice in its behalf. If it depends upon the home to render the results of Sabbath observances tangible, the Jew should take advantage of the Sabbath eve which, in most cases, is the only time when the home can be utilized for that purpose.

"Though the late Friday night services afford an opportunity for congregational worship to those who cannot attend synagogue on Sabbath morning, they do not constitute an ideal way of spending the Sabbath eve. That should be a time for family reunion. Away from the routine of work and the thousand and one distractions of clubs, organizations and entertainments, the members of the family might learn to know one another. It is then that parents should become acquainted with their children and children should exchange their experiences with their parents. The memories and impressions resulting from a Sabbath eve spent in this manner will have a far more permanent influence upon the happiness and character of Jews than the most successful Friday night services and lectures" (p. 445).

Innovation to Foster Unique Quality of Jewish Value System

Second, the foundation of Jewish education, as an education in human values instead of in facts and technics, must be laid in the home life and atmosphere. It is there that the child achieves the basis for whatever relevance and interest he can find in the studies of the religious school. That is especially the case with Jewish education, which, unlike general education, especially in the Diaspora, deals with facts and values which belong to an entirely different universe of discourse from the universe of discourse into which the child is thrown by the studies in the religious school. The fact that, despite the many years with Jewish education in America, it cannot be said to have achieved satisfactory results is not due to the lack of pedagogic ability on the part of the Jewish teacher and educator, but to lack of an educative Jewish atmosphere in the home. That condition would undoubtedly improve with the introduction of the Sabbath Eve Seder into the home.

Third, as a method of dealing with the problem of the extent to which it involves the conservation of religious practices as well as the spirit of Judaism as a whole, *innovation* is to be recommended. To quote one instance of the method of innovation, the institution of the *bat mitzvah*, which corrects the Jewish traditional attitude toward the religious status of the woman, is a form of amendment to a constitution.

Fourth, the spiritual primacy of the collective self-consciousness, which is Judaism's contribution to the humanization of man, would be underscored. In contrast with the Greek oracle "Know thyself," which is addressed to the individual, Hebraism's revelation in the Ten Commandments is addressed to the collective mind of the people of Israel. Thus Judaism, in keeping with Hillel's maxim, aims to have the individual not only know his individual needs but also the needs of the organic society to which he belongs, and without which he would not be able to meet his own individual needs in proper fashion. The sense of responsibility which the individual acquires through his belonging to an organic society like a family, clan, tribe or nation, adds the fourth dimension, holiness, which renders the other three dimensions authentic, viz: truth, goodness, creativity. Without the dimension of holiness, truth is likely to be rationalization, goodness to be not disinterested, and creativity to be for destructive ends.

Dimension of Holiness

On the other hand, it is the dimension of holiness which enables the human being to experience the reality of God with the same immediacy as he experiences the objects of the senses. This idea of God is in keeping with the oft repeated emphasis on God as being experienced when He is sought after. The prophet urged his people to "seek YHWH where He may be found and to call upon Him where He is near." Likewise the psalmist says: "YHWH is near unto all who call upon Him, to all who sincerely call upon Him." Were the prophet's and psalmist's words taken seriously, there would be an end to the misconception of religion as essentially concerned with the supernatural, the metaphysical, or the mystical aspect of reality. The meaning of the term *emunah* as faith, and therefore as the attitude of mind essentially associated with religion, would at last be recognized as a distortion of truth. On the other hand, as far as the Bible is concerned, the equivalent of the term "religion" is *hokhmah* — wisdom. (cf. Job 28:28).

The entire project of the Sabbath Eve Seder, however, depends for its success upon the cooperation of the rabbis. They would be only too happy to offer specific guidance on the way to conduct those Sedarim through their bulletins and special lectures, as well as through occasional demonstrations within their synagogues. The main problem is to see to it that whatever text is to be read should be provided with questions that would render it relevant.

Incidentally, that project might lead to the kind of mutual socialization among Jewish families that might help to foster Jewish collective consciousness, and that might attract to the synagogue those Jews who, for whatever reasons, have become alienated from it.

The Shabbat Seder Program

■ ■ ■ Joel Alpert

The Sabbath Eve Seder described below represents a new direction in Jewish education and family life. (The term "family" is used here to refer to any combination of one or more adults and one or more children.) The Seder program aims at providing an environment and context for the experiencing of Shabbat as a family and as part of a larger extended family, i.e., the synagogue or the community. It is hoped that the Seder program will regularly bring families together into these and other settings to celebrate Shabbat and Judaism. Most of all, we aim to create an environment of interaction where parent and child learn from each other, teach each other, and experience each other.

The program is meant to present Judaism to our students in an atmosphere outside of the classroom, while they are together with those with whom they regularly share life. It is hoped that through these programs families will grow together and that Judaism may come to play a regular part in their lives.

The Seder program is modeled on the Pesah Seder and is thus meant to be both an educational and a social program. The Pesah Seder itself contains many elements which make it an ideal model for this program: an ordered atmosphere that nevertheless includes a free-flowing question-and-answer format; a home- and family-based celebration which is open to all family members; and a series of rituals which surround a special meal.

This program is not intended as a program unto itself, although it could function in this way, but rather as a way of integrating families into a larger Jewish context, such as the synagogue, and as a way of preparing families so that they can apply what they learn and experience at the Seder to their Jewish life at home. In addition, the Seder program can be a component of the school curriculum with themes picked from areas of classroom study. A Seder could be used either to introduce an area of study or to conclude a study unit. It might also serve as a way of integrating parents into the ongoing program of the school.

The Seder experience includes a meal, a developing familiarity with Shabbat Eve rituals, and a study of a Jewish theme with topics chosen that lend themselves to exploration (not completion) in the course of a single evening. (See the detailed explanation of the Seder on Folk Tales below.)

The individual programs, designed for children aged eight to eleven and their families, run no more than two hours, including the meal. This age group seemed to work well because the students were old enough to verbalize their thoughts clearly with parents present but not so old that they did not want their parents present. The program has been tried successfully with some modification for younger and older groups. The success of the program depends not so much on the age-group involved or on the nature of the synagogue or school but rather upon the amount of family involvement that can be generated. A great deal of staff time is needed in preparing to get families to come and to share.

A Seder can be held in any setting but a large room or small auditorium works best. These provide enough space for the meal and for the participants to be able to move about as needed to work out the activities of the Seder. Our experience also indicates that the group size should be limited to allow as many people as possible to participate actively. Groups larger than twenty and less than forty seem to work best. Seder programs for as many as 150 people have been held. In a group this large, activities should be prepared which can involve a whole table of people together.

The staffing of a Seder program can consist of a rabbi and teacher, an educational director and teacher, a special team of teachers or individuals from the group, synagogue, or community, and, after a familiarity has been developed, different families. Whoever is chosen to staff the program, it is desirable that the program be led by the same personnel over a period of time. In this way, the type of consistency and familiarity that will help achieve the goals of the program can be developed.

Finally, it should be noted that this program developed out of discussions of the writings of Mordecai M. Kaplan. It is Kaplan who first wrote of the Seder idea as part of his goal of making the Sabbath a significant home experience for the Jewish people. Kaplan also wrote about the need for Jewish professionals to provide the members of the Jewish community with the ability to do things for themselves. This program is intended to be a step in that direction. Thus, in contrast to other similar program ideas, this program does not attempt to create an entire ritual as a substitute for a service, nor does it focus on a study-discussion format for learning. Rather, it places its emphasis on rituals that families can perform on their own and at home, and on learning through doing and sharing as part of a family and a community.

What follows is a description of the elements that can make up a Seder; a sample Seder; and outlines of other Sedarim that have been tried and tested. It is hoped that the reader will develop a much clearer idea of what this program is and how it works by reading and trying our outlines and then by developing others appropriate to the needs of other specific situations.

Elements of the Shabbat Seder

1) *A booklet is handed out which contains the Shabbat rituals and the "Four Questions."*
2) *Candle lighting.* Families are asked to bring Shabbat candles with them. The candles are lit, everyone closes his or her eyes, and we sing the blessing as a group.
3) *The "Four Questions."* To set the theme of the Seder, four questions about the theme are written by the coordinators. Four children are selected to read the questions. The questions may be answered later as part of an activity. They may also be used to generate a discussion at home after the Seder.
4) *Blessing the children.* We sing the "Sabbath Prayer" from *Fiddler on the Roof* together for the customary blessing of the children.
5) *Kiddush.* We use Sidney Greenberg's *Likrat Shabbat* for rituals. It is printed clearly, well translated, and contains a good transliteration.
6) *Motzi.* We sing this together with the song used by the National Federation of Temple Youth. Often, one of the Shabbat rituals or ritual objects (candles, hallah, hallah cover, wine) is explained by a coordinator. For good ritual explanations, see *The Jewish Catalog*; Philip Birnbaum, *A Book of Jewish Concepts*; Abraham Heller, *A Vocabulary of Jewish Life*; Abraham Millgram, *The Sabbath: A Day of Delight*; *Keeping Posted* 27:2 — an issue on the Sabbath; and the CCAR, *A Sabbath Manual.*
7) *The meal.* The options are to cater a meal, to have families bring "potluck" dinner, or to purchase coldcuts, bread, potato salad, cole slaw, and beverages. We have found the last option to be the most convenient and practical for our purposes.
8) *Birkhat Hamazon.* A shortened form, also taken from *Likrat Shabbat* by Sidney Greenberg.

9) *The question from home.* A question related to the theme is sent home as part of the Seder notice. The children each introduce all the family members, then give their answer to the question. Sometimes this may be done before the meal.

The home questions are used to initiate an exploration of the material as a family before the Seder. In addition, families are sometimes asked to bring an object. (See "Judaism and Art" and "The Jewish Idea of the Future.")

10) Theme activities. These may be readings, songs, discussions, or activities. For this type of group, activities—plays, word games, simulations—are the most successful. If more time is available, film or slides would be useful.

An available source for themes is *Keeping Posted* (Teacher's Edition), a monthly magazine published by the Union of American Hebrew Congregations, 838 Fifth Avenue, N.Y. 10021, which explores one theme a month.

11) *Closing song.* A short "Shabbat Shalom" song makes a good ending for the evening. With adult groups, a selection of *zemirot* might be included. These elements are best illustrated by the specific examples of Seders which follow.

12) *Additional material.* The booklet can also contain materials on the theme which are not used during the Seder. For example, common Hebrew terms and expressions might be listed and explained. A bibliography might be included. Also, books related to the theme might be displayed in the room.

SEDER I: Folk Tales

A. Four questions:
  1. What makes a folk tale Jewish?
  2. How do folk tales come about?
  3. Why do people like to tell folk tales?
  4. What do all folk tales have in common?
B. Questions from home: Bring a legend about your family.
C. Activities:
  1. Children present play of biblical folk tale "Tower of Babel" (See Appendix A).
  2. Parents present play based on midrash "The Tongue's Power" (See Appendix B).
  3. Listen together to a recording of "Bontscha the Silent," a short story in play form by Peretz.
  4. Sing "Dona, Dona."

5. Read introduction to Elie Wiesel's *Gates of the Forest*, which concludes, "God made man because he loves stories," or "God
made humans because God loves stories."
6. Folk tale films from other lands provide an interesting contrast.
This Seder program on folk tales was presented in the following way.
a. Welcome and explanation of the Seder concept, if this is the first
program.
b. A short Shabbat song or two as a warm-up.
c. Introduction of families. The child whose class is involved introduces
his or her family.
d. Blessings over candles, wine, and bread, and the asking of the four
questions. The kids ask the questions and, if any of the rituals
are explained, we also have one of the kids present the explanation.

MEAL

BIRKAT HAMAZON

e. Read introduction from Wiesel's *Gates of the Forest* to set the tone for
the activities that follow and for the answering of the home
question.
f. Call on each family to tell their family legend.
g. Discussion can now follow briefly on e. and f., as well as on the four
questions.
h. Have parents and children go off to corners of the room to prepare
their presentation of a folk tale (see Appendix A for children's
tale and Appendix B for parents').
i. Presentation—this helps to personalize the lesson and also to get people
up and moving before the last activities, which are more serious.
j. Listen to recording of "Bontscha the Silent" and allow for reactions.
k. End with explanation and singing of "Dona, Dona."

Folk tale films can be available. We used them for those who came
early as well as for those who stayed late. They can be used during the
Seder if time allows. They probably fit best just before the last song. They
could also be used in the school as a follow-up to the Seder.

One additional activity that could be used in the school to conclude
is to have students write their own folk tales and perhaps present them
for the rest of the school or for parents.

Appendix A to Seder I: THE TOWER OF BABEL

A Biblical Tale
Scene: A crowd of people in the land of Shinar.

Narrator:	Once upon a time, there were no nations and all the people of the earth lived and worked together. Everyone spoke the same language. One day, someone had an idea.
Person 1:	Let's build a city!
Person 2:	In this city, we can build a tower!
Person 3:	With this tower we can reach the sky!
Person 4:	It can save us from being scattered all over the world!
Person 5:	We can become as great as the Lord!
Crowd:	Let's get the bricks! Where's my shovel? I'll start making the mortar! Let's get going!

(The people start building a tower.)

Narrator:	The Lord came down to look at the city and the tower which the people of the world were building. The Lord said:
Voice of God:	If, as one people with one language for all, this is how they behave, then they can do anything they want to do! I will go down and give them different languages! Then they won't understand each other when they talk.

(The people begin babbling and fighting with one another.)

Narrator:	And so, the Lord gave them different languages. The people could not understand each other. They disagreed and they argued and they could not build the city. The people scattered over the face of the earth. The place where the people tried to build their tower became known as Babel because there the Lord mixed up their speech. It was as if the people babbled.
Curtain	

Appendix B to Seder I: THE TONGUE'S POWER

A Midrashic Folk Tale
Scene: The king's palace. The king lies gravely ill.

Court Doctors:	Your Majesty, you are gravely ill. The only thing that could save your life is the milk of a lioness.
King:	Then we shall offer a huge reward to whomever will go and get the milk.

Narrator:	Only one man, a servant, volunteered for the dangerous mission. At the peril of his life, he obtained a jug of the precious milk and started back to the palace. But, weary from his ordeal, he decided to rest before going to the king. As he slept, the parts of his body started to dispute, each claiming credit for the feat.
Brain:	It was my cunning that captured the lioness in her lair.
Hands:	But we did the milking.
Feet:	We brought you to the den.
Heart:	If it had not been for my courage, none of you would have arrived there.
Tongue:	What could you have done without me? *(All the parts of the body laugh in scorn.)* Wait and you'll see what I mean.
Narrator:	Arriving before the king, the servant was strangely silent. His tongue stuck to the roof of his mouth. When it finally loosened, he was horrified to hear what his tongue said.
Servant:	Your Majesty, here is the milk of a dog.
King:	What? For such impertinence, you will lose your head!
Narrator:	The servant was seized and thrown into prison to await execution. All the parts of the body trembled in terror, but the tongue remained calm.
Tongue:	I told you that you were helpless without me. Now I shall save you. *(Tongue calls to the guard.)*
Servant:	Before I die, let me see the king and beg his pardon. *(Before king)* Your Majesty, I was so frightened that I misspoke myself. I said dog when I meant lioness. I beg you, inspect the milk, test it.
Narrator:	This was done, and both the king and the servant were saved. The king heaped rewards on the servant, and the parts of the body gave the tongue its due.
Parts of Body:	Death and life are in the power of the tongue *(Prov. 18:21).*

SEDER II: What's in a Name?

A. Four questions
   1. Why are our names important to us?
   2. What makes a name Jewish?
   3. Why do we have Hebrew and English names?
   4. Why do people change their names?

B. Home Question: What does your family name mean? Where does it come from?
C. Activities:
1. Cut out magazine pictures – have people try to "name" the person or animal in the picture. Discuss Adam naming the animals.
2. Give Hebrew names to those who have none. (Use Jonathan Kolatch, *The Complete Dictionary of English and Hebrew Names*.)
3. Try to list all the names of God (for those who don't write on Shabbat, cards may be prepared in advance with God's names).

Examples: *El Shaddai, Elohim, Adonai, YHWH, Av Ha-Rahamim, Ribbono Shel Olam, Ha-Makom, Avinu Malkenu, Ro'eh Yisrael.* Talk about what these names convey about God.

4. Give former names of people who have changed their names. Guess who they are now. Talk about reasons for changing your name. Examples: Milton Schapiro ... Milton Schapp, David Green ... David Ben-Gurion, Cassius Clay ... Muhammad Ali, Mosheh ben Maimon ... Maimonides; Rambam

SEDER III: Heroes

A. Four questions:
1. What makes a hero different from other people?
2. What makes a hero Jewish?
3. Who is the greatest Jewish hero?
4. What kind of sandwiches are we having for dinner? *(We had "hero" sandwiches that night.)*
B. From home: Who is your favorite Jewish hero?
C. Activities:
1. If done at Hanukah, a discussion of the Maccabees and a Hanukah song (like "Mi Yemallel") set a good tone.
2. Activity comparing story of Utnapishtim (hero of Gilgamesh Epic) and Noah. (References are included in Appendix to Seder III.)
3. Each person names one character trait they think a hero should have. (Non-writing groups should make a list anticipating suggestions – *Roget's Thesaurus* is helpful.)
4. Play "What's My Line?" – have people pretend to be "not- so-famous" Jews, and have others guess their occupations. Some suggestions: Solomon Schiff – the rabbi for the Miami Dolphins. Regina Jonas – Germany's first woman rabbi, who was killed during the Holocaust. Morris Lichtenstein – founder of

Jewish Science, a movement which kept American Jews in the 1920s from converting to Christian Science.
5. A film or slides or discussion about Masada is also appropriate.

Appendix to Seder III: References

Heidel, A. *The Babylonian Genesis*. Chicago: University of Chicago Press, 1963.
_____. *The Gilgamesh Epic and Old Testament Parallels*. Chicago: University of Chicago Press, 1963.
Pritchard, James, ed. *Ancient Near Eastern Texts Relating to the Old Testament*, Princeton: Princeton University Press, 1955.
Sarna, Nahum. *Understanding Genesis*, New York: The Jewish Theological Seminary of America, 1966.
Speiser, E.A. *Genesis*. Garden City, New York: Doubleday, 1964.

SEDER IV: Happiness

A. Four questions:
   1. What makes each of us happy?
   2. What is the Jewish idea of happiness?
   3. How can we be happy in a world full of war, hunger, and poverty?
   4. Why have a Seder about happiness?
B. Home question: What one thing makes your family happy?
C. Activities:
   1. Each family gets a "Jewish happiness" topic to explain. Examples: "Love your neighbor as yourself." "The creation of the world." "Doing mitzvot." "Who is happy? He who rejoices when the world goes well for others." "Shabbat." "Simhat Torah." "Births, weddings."
   2. Debate: One adult and one child (not from same family) on each side. RESOLVED: You *can* be happy in a world full of hunger, war, and poverty.
   3. Songs: *Hineh Mah Tov* (with different melodies), "Happiness" from the musical *You're a Good Man, Charlie Brown*.
   4. Box—this is happiness—guess what's inside. The actual contents are bread and Torah. Discuss why they are both necessary for happiness.

SEDER V: Jerusalem
(Recommended for older children.)

A. Four questions:
1. Why is Jerusalem different from all other cities?
2. All other cities belong to one people or nation—why is Jerusalem claimed by three faiths?
3. All other cities are interesting, so why do we end our Pesah Sedarim every year with the wish "Next Year in Jerusalem"?
4. Many other cities have walls, but why does Jerusalem have a Wailing Wall?

Please note: It is extremely important that these questions be answered as part of the activity section of this Seder. Question #2 lends itself to a debate with people representing the three faiths that claim Jerusalem. One technique that will work for the other questions is to write out in advance several possible answers for each question—some right and some wrong—and then have each family read their card and discuss what is written on it.

B. Home activity: Have each family bring a wish to place in the "Wall" and explain why they brought that wish. (Make sure that you explain the custom of putting wishes in the cracks of the Wailing Wall before you proceed with this activity.)

C. Activities:
1. Share experiences of being in Jerusalem.
2. Slide and tape show with history and legends about Jerusalem.
3. Songs about Jerusalem—"Jerusalem of Gold," "*Hakotel*," "*Lakh Yerushalayim*," "*Yerushalayim*," etc.

D. Two important resources are:
1. Zev Vilnay's *Legends of Jerusalem* (Jewish Publication Society).
2. "Jerusalem: Why are Nations in an Uproar?" *Keeping Posted* 17, 5 (Union of American Hebrew Congregations).

SEDER VI: Jewish Life in Eastern Europe

A. Four questions:
1. What was the shtetl?
2. Why were the Jews forced to be separate?
3. Why are there no shtetls in Eastern Europe today?
4. Is there a shtetl in America?
B. Home Question: Which of your relatives remember the shtetl? Where are they from? (At Seder, hang map with flags and family names, illustrating where our ancestors came from.)

C. Activities:
1. Hold up bagel—is this bread "Jewish?" Why is Eastern European food thought to be Jewish food in America? Note close ties.
2. Sing Yiddish song.
3. Get parents to tell stories from the shtetl.
4. Word associations with pogrom, Yiddish, shtetl.
5. Families are told that they are in Eastern Europe and things are becoming difficult. Have them choose whether they would stay in Russia, go to Palestine, or go to America. Elicit values upon which decision depends. (America—hope for wealth, sense of adventure. Palestine—Zionist commitment, pioneer spirit. Russia—security, familiarity, known quantity.)

SEDER VII: Judaism and Art

A. Four questions:
1. What is art?
2. What is Jewish art?
3. Is all art created by Jews Jewish art?
4. The Ten Commandments say "You shall not make a graven image." What has that meant to Jewish art?
B. Home Question: Bring with you some object that you think is Jewish art.
C. Activities:
1. Dramatize the Golden Calf story. (See Appendix following).
2. Bring pictures of unusual Jewish art objects—guess what they are and where they are from.
3. Is a painting of a Jew by Rembrandt Jewish art? (Bring illustration.)
4. Vote: Are these things Jewish art? A Jewish joke, a ritual object, a book (the Bible), an advertisement for a Jewish movie or play, the synagogue you are in, etc.
5. For older groups, the film *The Hebrew Script* talks about Jewish calligraphy.

Appendix to Seder VII: THE GOLDEN CALF

Narrator: The story takes place while Moses is on Mt. Sinai writing down the words of God. The Israelites grow restless waiting for him to return.

Israelite #1: Where is Moses? Why hasn't he returned to us yet?

Israelite #2:	He sure has been up there for a long time. I don't think that he's coming back.
Israelite #3:	Let's get Moses' brother Aaron to make us a god to go before us.
Israelite #4: (spokesman to Aaron)	Aaron, make us a god. We don't know what has happened to Moses, the man who brought us up from Egypt.
Aaron:	Take the golden rings from your wives and sons and daughters and bring them to me.
Narrator:	The people collected the rings and brought them to Aaron. He made a molten calf from them with an engraving tool, and said to the people:
Aaron:	This is your god who brought you out of Egypt.
Narrator:	The people prepared a feast. They sat down to eat and drink before the calf, and to worship before it. Meanwhile, God alerted Moses to what the people had done. Moses returned and was very angry.
Moses:	You people have sinned a very great sin by making for yourselves a god of gold. Never do it again!

SEDER VIII: The Jewish Idea of the Future

A. Four questions:
  1. What is the Messiah?
  2. How will Judaism be different in the year 2000?
  3. What is your hope for Judaism in the future?
  4. What might our synagogue be like in the year 2000?
B. Home Question: What would you put in a Jewish time capsule? If possible, bring the object to the Seder.
C. Activities:
  1. Discuss idea of "Messiah."
  2. Decide if these are good wishes for the messianic age: "Lion and lamb lie down together." "No one shall be afraid." "The Temple will be rebuilt and sacrifices restored." "Everyone will study Torah." "Sleep will be unnecessary." "Everyone will believe in one God."
  3. Have someone claim to be the Messiah who will fulfill all the wishes in #2. Try to get people to believe in him or her.
  4. Sing "Eliahu Ha-Navi."

SEDER IX: *The Jewish Calendar*

A. Four questions:
  1. Why is this 5745 and 1985?
  2. Why is there often an extra month in the Hebrew calendar?
  3. Why is the Hebrew calendar based on the moon and the secular calendar based on the sun?
  4. What calendar is used in Israel?

B. At Home: Bring Hebrew/English calendar. (For those who forget, you can obtain many from Jewish funeral homes, etc.)

C. Activities:
  1. Using Arthur Spier's *The Comprehensive Hebrew Calendar*, calculate Hebrew birth dates of children in program. (Give out cards with this information.)
  2. Explain that Shabbat begins in evening—Hebrew day begins at sundown, not midnight. Highlight difference.
  3. Explain Rosh Hodesh—celebration of beginning of each new month—parallel Rosh Hashanah.
  4. Make chart to convert from Hebrew year to secular year and do some date conversions: (5)745 + 240 = (1)985
  5. Calendar exercises: Have people find secular dates for Yom Kippur in two consecutive years. (Calendars usually have two Septembers.) Find Hebrew date for American holiday. Have each child find his/her Hebrew birthday this year. Find Rosh Hodesh of some Jewish month—mention names of other Hebrew months.

SEDER X: *World Hunger*

This is a "non-Seder." A letter is sent to families asking that instead of joining together for the Shabbat Seder, each family donate the cost of the meal to the local Jewish contact organization for world hunger.

With the letter send the article "Torah, World Hunger and Us" from *Keeping Posted* 20,6 (1975), the issue on World Hunger. Families are asked to read and discuss the article together at home.

SEDER XI: *Hanukah Seder*

A. Four questions:
  1. What relationship exists between the dreidel, the menorah, and the festival of Hanukah?

2. Why do we eat latkes while Israelis eat jelly donuts during Hanukah? (This refers to the use of *oil* and its place in the Hanukah story.)
        3. Who were the Maccabees?
        4. What is a miracle?
    B. Home project: Bring in a gift for someone at the Seder or for someone some place else. Be prepared to discuss why that particular gift and person were chosen.
    C. Theme activities:
        1. A Hanukah sing down.
        2. Explain the meaning of the dreidel and how to play with it. Allow some time for play.
        3. Ask people to make a choice between having a Christmas tree with gifts, a menorah, or both. Have them explain their choice.
        4. Display and use Hanukiyot made in school.
        5. Share the home project.
    D. Hanukah songs.

SEDER XII: *Israel and America*

(Works better with older children)
    A. Four questions:
        1. What do Israel and America have in common?
        2. How are Israel and America different?
        3. Where do you feel more Jewish?
        4. Where do you feel more at home?
    B. Home activity: Bring two objects to the Seder—one of which is a symbol of Israel and one of which is a symbol of America.
    C. Activities:
        1. Have each family choose where they want to live and discuss why. Which country—America or Israel? Which city?
        2. Have the family name American and Israeli heroes. Compare and contrast their choices.
        3. Film: *America I Love You*. (This film presents a lively often humorous cross section of American Jews as they see themselves in a series of informal "man-in-the-street interviews." The two Israelis who made the film for Israeli TV posed questions about Jewish identity and assimilation, insecurity vis-à-vis non-Jews, and attitudes toward Israel versus the United States. The total effect is both entertaining and sharply thought-provoking.)
        4. Plan an activity or activities which allow the families to deal with the study of American versus Israeli history. One tech-

nique would be to hold up an American history textbook and a copy of the Hebrew Bible, and discuss the implications of each for the study of history. In addition, some discussion of the role of archaeology would be appropriate.

5. Songs—An interesting activity would be to provide the group with the words of the national anthem of each country and then to discuss the implications. (This activity may appeal more to adults.)

Other Seder ideas: Jewish foods, Jewish costumes, Purim, Hanukah, Tu B'shevat, Soviet Jewry, women in Judaism, Jewish law, Jewish humor, the Haggadah, Zionism, Jewish languages, life cycle, Judaism & Christianity, local Jewish community.

CREATIVE READINGS

Examples of creative readings that can be used to introduce and explain Shabbat rituals:

Candles—Hadlakat Nerot

We light two Shabbat candles. They represent *shamor* (keep, guard) and *zakhor* (remember)—first words of the commandments concerning Shabbat. They also symbolize the unity underlying all apparent duality, such as man and woman, body and soul, speech and silence, creation and revelation.

Waving the hands around the candles serves to usher in the Shabbat as the light of the Shabbat fills the room and surrounds the person; it symbolizes the culmination of the six days of creation into the seventh day of rest; it draws the warmth and light inside oneself. (adapted from *The Jewish Catalogue*)

Kiddush

The Sabbath wine is a symbol of the wholeness of life. There are times when we drink from bitter cups, yet there are also times when we savor the sweetness and joy that exalt life.

Thus our *Kiddush* points to the recognition that life is both joy and sorrow. We resolve to affirm and accept them both, and so all of life. This affirmation and acceptance provide the true happiness of which this cup speaks. Let us then raise our Sabbath cup to the fullness that is life. (From *A Common Service*)

Bread — Hamotzi

Integral to the Jewish tradition is respect for bread because it is the staff of life.

Therefore, the sages taught, one is not to throw it around, use it as a tool, or waste it.

Since life is holy, bread has a kind of holiness attached to it. We therefore bless our God for bringing forth bread from the earth. (adapted from Shonie B. Levi)

Conclusion

These examples of Sedarim represent some of the many options available. Clearly the application of this program idea is as limitless as the human imagination. A series of Sedarim could bring new life and meaning to a backyard or communal Sukkah. A creative option for a bar/bat mitzvah might be a Shabbat morning brunch Seder prepared by the bar or bat mitzvah. A multi-generational seder of Jewish life as it has changed in this century could bring together age groups that do not often enough mix and yet who have much to offer each other. The Pesah Seder might become less mechanical and more meaningful. Similarly, many other events of the Jewish life and calendar cycles might become more meaningful and appealing if they were based on a model that was less formal and mechanical than what most of Judaism has become in recent times. The Seder model may be one element in a return to Jewish living and education for those whom we fear we will lose through assimilation and apathy. And those who presently care and participate may find new levels of enjoyment and learning that were not previously available to them.

A Practical Guide in the Formation of a Havurah

■ ■ ■ Steven Stroiman

Fifteen years ago, the term "havurah" was virtually absent from most of our vocabularies. Today, we use it as some kind of exotic elixir to heal the woes of our troubled Jewish community. Just pour some of it over a synagogue, sprinkle it on a singles group at the neighborhood Jewish community center, or baste it lightly over a lodge, and in seconds you have a havurah. Unfortunately, such indiscriminate use of the term can leave a somewhat bitter aftertaste and can drive away some of its more serious devotees. What is called for is a recipe with certain basic ingredients which can be adapted to specific tastes. Though it may be unfair to compare a havurah to a kugel, we can perhaps emulate this favorite among Jewish culinary delights. Its contents may vary considerably (potato or noodle), as well as its effect on the palate (salty or sweet). Yet, the same basic guidelines are followed in making a kugel, and no one would ever mistake it for anything but a kugel.

Definition

Before looking at the ingredients which go into the formation of a havurah, we must first understand what is meant by the term. If we were to consult a Hebrew-English dictionary, the English equivalent would be "fellowship," which would not bring us too much closer to what a havurah is all about. Put in a more practical way, a havurah is a small group of individuals who meet informally on a regular basis to do Jewish things together. Havurot tend to be self-directed in the sense of having no assigned or paid leader; leadership comes from within the group. In a related manner, such a group is usually egalitarian, in that men and women are accorded the same status regarding ritual functions (e.g., both are counted in a minyan and both can receive an aliyah). A closer look at this general definition of a havurah can put some of its basic elements into sharper focus.

BEFORE THE FIRST MEETING: SOME INITIAL CONSIDERATIONS

Membership

An initial question to ask regarding this definition is, "Who's interested?" Friends, acquaintances from the office or from some organization? Singles, couples, families, or what? What's better—a homogeneous or heterogeneous group in terms of age, socioeconomic standing, etc.? There is no clear-cut rule which can be applied in determining the composition of a havurah. However, a group will often build a foundation based on the common interests and needs of its members. In other words, while it may not be unusual for college undergraduates and married couples with young children to plan and enjoy a holiday meal together, their primary interests in belonging to an ongoing group such as a havurah may vary significantly. Generally, what happens in forming this type of group is that individuals will speak with others who they feel have similar interests and who have common backgrounds. Each of those contacted may in turn invite a friend or acquaintance to a first meeting.

Starting a havurah with friends does not necessarily put a group at an advantage. A havurah is not a friendship group, whose major purpose in getting together is to share each other's company; the activity in such a group is usually secondary in importance. On the other hand, a havurah is also not a formal institution whose primary reason for meeting is to accomplish some task. Somewhere in between is the havurah. While its primary purpose is to get together for Jewish functions and activities, an important by-product of this interaction is fellowship, a camaraderie which may develop into a friendship. Havurah members—haverim—may become good friends while also retaining their own sphere of close friends outside the group.

Size

Once the people have been contacted and are ready to meet, a second factor now comes into focus—the size of the havurah. This is sometimes an overlooked and difficult aspect to deal with in our society. Having been raised on "the bigger, the better" formula for most of our lives, many of us have fled its undesirable consequences of being overcrowded, impersonal, and sterile. We have raised a new banner, "small is beautiful," and have invoked its humanistic potentials. Yet, being novices in this arena, we're not quite sure how "smallness" can bring about involvement, meaningfulness, and interpersonal relationships. Can one point to specific numbers which would constitute a small group? Without going into theories of group dynamics, it is estimated that approximately ten to twenty-five people would comprise a manageable size for a havurah in terms of its purposes and activities. This is not to say that groups with more or less would automatically be at a disadvantage. It is merely a guideline with which to work. One havurah used a very practical yardstick to measure the size of their group—it was decided that the group would consist of no more than the number of people who could fit comfortably in the living rooms of their homes.

Meeting Place and Location

While meeting in a synagogue or hall may be preferable to some of the people, the tendency of many havurot is to get together in one another's homes. It is this aspect which lends itself most to the informal quality mentioned in the definition of a havurah. Returning Judaism to the home has its symbolic as well as real life connotations. The comfort of familiar surroundings along with the soft, rounded features of the furniture convey a sense of warmth and security. Reclining on a couch or stretching out on the carpet are examples of the ease with which people can relax in this kind of setting.

Like many of the "ingredients" being discussed in the formation of a havurah, that of location cannot be pinned down to any hard and fast rule. However, a reasonable proximity to each other's homes is a factor which may be considered in the beginning. Since membership is voluntary and is not based on convenience in terms of time and effort, time for travel may be expected up to a point. If meetings are expected to rotate among the members' homes, what usually happens is that meetings are scheduled less often at those homes which are farthest from the central point. Nobody likes to "shlep," regardless of the importance of a meeting, especially if there are obstacles (such as the weather, a malfunctioning car, or pressing errands) which impede one's efforts. Also, distance becomes more of a factor if the attractiveness—the appeal—of the group wanes for the individual. The time that would normally be used for travel to and from the havurah meeting would be used for "more interesting or pressing" things for such a person.

THE FIRST (AND SUBSEQUENT) MEETING(S)

How to Begin

Now that people are seated comfortably in the living room of someone's home for the first meeting, what is supposed to happen? There seem to be so many things to discuss. Yet, how do you start and what do you bring up first? Obviously, if everyone is not acquainted with one another, introductions and a brief sharing of background information are appropriate ways to begin. Because of the informal atmosphere which is intended for such a group, it is preferable to start as naturally as possible, without superimposing some structured activity or game format upon the meeting. In other words, people coming together for the first time have concerns and needs which they want to discuss with the others. They want to see if others have similar concerns. If this is the case, then the group begins to take on a sense of purpose for those people. Whether stated or not, everyone has some expectations for a new group like this, and the time to begin discussing them is during this initial meeting.

Making Decisions by Consensus

Some of the issues which are recommended for discussion during the first (and subsequent) meeting(s) are those that affect the group's immediate functioning, such as the areas mentioned above (membership, size, meeting place, location). Though these may have been mentioned among individuals during the "recruitment" phase, it is important that they be discussed with everyone present. Reaching a general understanding and decision together about such matters is not only necessary but vital to the kind of group being formed. It was mentioned earlier that people seek involvement in a havurah, and one direct way of achieving it is through the groping and tugging which take place as decisions are being made. Decisions by consensus require an understanding and acceptance by everyone if many of the positive aspects of a havurah are to be realized. This does not mean that people are to be "yes men" and acquiesce. Nor does it mean that unanimity is expected. Rather, opinions may differ and are to be taken into account when deciding by consensus.

SPECIFIC EXPECTATIONS AND CONCERNS

Attendance

One guideline to take seriously during the early period of the group is that assumptions should not be made. Misunderstandings may arise because something may not have been discussed or agreed upon by everyone. One such assumption which should be clarified in the beginning is that of attendance. Is it expected that everyone attends all the meetings? What if someone – child or adult – comes but does not want to participate, for some reason? The answers have to come from the members themselves. It is recommended, however, that the meetings be scheduled so that all the members can attend them.

Frequency of Meetings

Related to the above issue of attendance is the frequency with which meetings are to take place. Generally, a comfortable period between the first and second meeting is about two or three weeks. Meeting less frequently than once per month or more often than every other week may be pushing or pulling things too much in the beginning. As the group progresses beyond the first couple of meetings, the members may want to set aside part of the next meeting to plan for the next two or three months. The types of get-togethers (which are discussed in more detail below) should include holiday celebrations and possibly some community events. At this planning meeting, calendars and/or datebooks should be brought so that the dates and places are mutually acceptable.

Autonomy

Another expectation to discuss is the level of autonomy the group is to have. If the havurah is part of a synagogue, at what points do the members want the group to be involved with synagogue functions? Is the rabbi to be involved? If so, to what degree? The members have to find a balance which reflects their needs for such a dual affiliation. The same applies to a havurah which is not affiliated with a synagogue or organization. If some of the members belong to other groups which may overlap in their activities, it is possible for the groups to complement one another. For example, a youngster may teach the havurah a new Israeli dance which he learned from his youth group.

It is not to be expected that a havurah will provide everything that every member wants. Turning to some other group or organization for the purpose of supplementing (or complementing) the havurah's activities should not be looked upon as a shortcoming of the group. On the contrary, such exposure to outside resources can benefit and enrich the havurah. However, a word of caution is necessary—autonomy requires a certain degree of independence as well as a purpose separate from that of other groups. It is important that a havurah be distinctive and unique to its members, that it provide things which other groups cannot provide (or cannot do as well). Such examples are usually in the realm of the qualitative, like a feeling of belonging, a sense of community, an exciting air of really living Jewishly, etc. Of course, the descriptions do not have to be limited to one's feelings. Specifics, like the way the havurah celebrates holidays and life cycle events, how it learns Hebrew, or the manner in which it integrates the weekly Torah portion with contemporary issues, can point out the special qualities of one's havurah.

Focusing on What the Havurah Is (Rather than What it is Not)

One of the major concerns of many people forming a havurah is often that this group is not to be like the synagogue or fund-raising organization to which they have belonged or with which they are familiar. It is not to be controlled by a handful of individuals; it is not to have its religious functions run by one person with a congregation of passive recipients; it is not to compartmentalize families into such boxes as Junior Congregation or Adult Education; and the list goes on *ad infinitum*.

While this "adversary" approach may be helpful in the beginning in terms of distinguishing the havurah from other groups, the havurah must eventually move from this position to one expressing a positive identity. Instead of dwelling on what the group does not do, which does not help generate alternative ways of responding to a situation, the members can start to think about what the group can do. For example, if there is not to be a "rabbi" leading the havurah, then what can the members do in place of such an approach? If the group decides that it wants to develop a sense of shared leadership among all (or most) of its members, then the next question to ask is, "How?" They may experiment with a number of approaches such as having the host(s) (at whose home the meeting is being held) serve as the chairperson(s) for the meeting. Or planning sessions and/or other activities can be done in small groups or with partners in order to give people more opportunities to participate. Another method is to have each person (or family) assume responsibility for the preparation and presentation of some topic (or an aspect of a group activity such as the food, songs, chairs and tables, theme material, etc.) After a specified period of time, the group might want to discuss and evaluate these approaches and their effectiveness (or lack of it).

Throughout this discussion of the expectations and concerns of the people in a havurah, some specific issues have been raised. Obviously, it is far from being a complete list, nor does it necessarily reflect issues which a particular group may feel are more important. Other issues that may arise include the following: the tension between the needs of the individual and the needs of the group; the varying level(s) of Jewish observance among the members; the relative emphasis that the group places upon cultural activities, religious observances, and social gatherings; the balance between activities geared to the needs of the children and those directed at the adults' needs; and the group's ability to adapt to changes.

As the havurah matures, the members will decide which issues should be pursued and which will take care of themselves over the course of time. And if the members learn to deal with the more difficult areas (such as personality problems) in addition to programming and procedural issues, then the group will enjoy a productive and fulfilling venture which may continue for many years.

TYPES OF HAVURAH ACTIVITIES AND MEETINGS

Though a major segment of this paper has dealt with expectations and concerns, the havurah need not spend meeting after meeting discussing them. If that were the case, not too many members would remain. In fact, it is recommended that as early as the third meeting the group should stop "discussing" and start "doing." Below are some suggestions for activities in which the members can be involved.

Shabbat Dinner (and Oneg Shabbat)

If this is to be the group's first activity of this type (other than a discussion meeting), the plans for such an evening should be rather simple and easy in order to allow the members the opportunity to interact informally with one another. Its purpose should not be an intensive Erev Shabbat experience, which requires a degree of planning, understanding, and comfort working together as a group that has not yet been attained at this stage of its development. Rather, a potluck dinner in which everyone can contribute something, along with some Shabbat melodies and ritual observances (e.g., candle lighting, kiddush, motzi), generally do not entail hours of planning and prior discussion. The extent of Shabbat ritual observances depends on the backgrounds of the members and their comfort with the various customs. This, in fact, could possibly be the focal point of discussion after dinner (along with the role of Shabbat in the lives of the members). Or, again depending on their backgrounds, discussion could center around the Torah portion of the week, which would require some preparation in terms of reading (and understanding) the particular *parashah*. An Oneg Shabbat might also consist of singing and sharing songs (from summer camp days or from one's youth group experiences), reminiscing and swapping humorous incidents, learning some Israeli dances, bringing in poetry or a short story (which some of the members may have written), or anything else which would contribute to this kind of informal, positive experience.

Celebration of Holidays

As was mentioned above, it is generally preferable for a havurah to have a Shabbat dinner and Oneg Shabbat before it plans for a holiday celebration because of the relative ease and simplicity involved. Again, this depends on the type of group and cannot apply to every havurah. It is also suggested that planning first be done for a festive holiday rather than for the more solemn holidays (such as Rosh Hashanah, Yom Kippur, Tisha B'Av, etc.). Passover, Hanukah, Purim, Sukkot, Simhat Torah, etc. are especially good for havurot consisting of families because of their appeal to the children. Everyone, including the children, can be involved in some way in the planning. A meeting should be set aside to discuss and coordinate all the aspects of the holiday at least three weeks in advance in order to allow time for people to learn, practice, obtain material, meet again, or whatever is necessary for such a preparation. The following are some elements to take into consideration:

THEME: In what ways, for example, can the members deal with the concept of religious freedom during the holiday of Hanukah? There are numerous options – a creative service, skits, a debate, a movie, a play. Brainstorming during the planning meeting(s) can produce innovative ideas and approaches.

CUSTOMS: Which customs does the havurah want to observe and how are they to be done? Does the group, for instance, want to observe the custom of *matanot le-evyonim*, distributing gifts to the poor during Purim? If so, what should be sent and to whom? What about the havurah instituting its own customs, such as baking its own matzot before Passover?

FOOD: What are the typical holiday recipes and special foods? Who is to bring what? Some research into some Sephardic dishes can bring about interesting changes in the traditional menu.

SONGS, DANCES: What holiday songs can be learned? Perhaps someone knows a different melody to a familiar song which he/she can introduce. Instruments of all kinds – guitar, clarinet, violin, recorder, etc. – should be brought to enhance the spirit of the occasion. Also, it is important that copies of new songs be distributed (with transliteration included for those who may not be able to read Hebrew) so that everyone can learn and participate in the singing.

SERVICES: What kind of service does the group want to hold—traditional or innovative or one with elements of both? Does the group want to do an entire service, parts of it, or nothing at all? These questions have to be dealt with during a planning meeting and determined before the holiday celebration.

BASIC LOGISTICS: How many chairs are needed? Who can pick up the *lulavim* and *etrogim*? What about holding the celebration outside in a backyard or in a park? Is it better to have the skits before or after the meal? Dozens of such questions will arise throughout the planning, which is why plenty of time is needed to get things coordinated.

Study Meeting

This type of meeting can revolve around a particular topic chosen by the group during a brainstorming session, or the members may want to meet in small groups for part of the meeting to discuss different topics and reconvene for something else during the second half of the meeting. Whether gathering as a whole group or in small groups, the duration of the study of the topic(s) should be discussed. Does the havurah want to have a study meeting once each month (i.e., so that every other meeting is to focus on the chosen topic)? Approximately how many sessions should the topic span, and what if the group wants to continue (or discontinue) beyond those sessions?

There is a vast range of topics from which to choose, including traditional texts (the Bible, the Midrash, aspects of halakhah), current political issues (the Middle East, Jews in America, Soviet Jewry, Jews in other lands), history (shtetl life, the Holocaust, Zionism), and customs (the Jewish life cycle, the calendar, worship, symbols), to name a few in a seemingly inexhaustible list of subjects. Resources can be obtained from the libraries of the members as well as from local public, university, synagogue, and Jewish school libraries. People in the community and in organizations can also serve as resources—for example, the Anti-Defamation League, the Student Struggle for Soviet Jewry, the Hillel Foundation, the Israeli Consulate, etc.

As was mentioned earlier, it is important for everyone to participate in these study sessions, including children and adults. Each family can prepare a segment to present, and the material can be presented in various ways (and on different levels). The presentations should be interesting and should be able to hold the attention of the group. Discussions which follow may possibly be geared more to the adults and the older youngsters. The younger children should be given the option to leave the room if they do not want to stay and listen. (It should be noted that if the children choose to go to another room, they should not disturb the discussion going on.

Services (Tefillot)

Thus far, services have been discussed within the context of holiday celebrations. However, this does not mean that services cannot be conducted apart from other activities. In fact, there are numerous occasions in which services can be the primary component of a meeting. On Shabbat evening or morning, the members may want to get together primarily to *daven* with one another. The beautiful *Havdalah* service, in which the group can gather to bid farewell to the *"Shabbos* Queen" by using the various symbolic objects, is another excellent time to get together. A Sunday morning or evening may provide an opportunity to be involved in the format of the daily services.

Within a havurah, it may be found that some members are familiar with the traditional prayers while others have had little exposure to them. It should not be assumed, however, that the more knowledgeable members are to be the only ones who conduct services. There are several ways in which the less informed individuals can be involved, such as leading the group in one of the prayers (in English or even in Hebrew), perhaps accompanying the group with an instrument during certain melodies, typing up the services (if they are compiled by the havurah), bringing an appropriate reading or prayer or song to share, or just helping with some of the other logistics involved (e.g., distributing *siddurim*, transporting the Torah scroll). The members can learn about traditional worship at study meetings and during the course of other meetings and activities. Services can thus be an active, participatory experience for everyone.

Community Involvement

There are dozens of ways for a havurah to get involved in Jewish and general community events. Examples of the activities the group can do throughout the year include: substituting for some of the Christian staff at a neighborhood hospital on Christmas Eve; conducting a Seder for the Jewish elderly; building a float for the *Yom Ha-atzma'ut* parade; participating in a Soviet Jewry rally; and presenting aspects of Jewish folklore and customs at a city-wide ethnic cultural program. Involvement in these kinds of activities often elicits a feeling of pride and a sense of cohesiveness in the havurah.

Trips

Trips are another way of having the havurah involved in the wider community. They can range from a few hours to several days. An afternoon tour of a Jewish museum (or a general museum with a display of Jewish interest), an evening at a neighborhood Jewish center to see a play or hear a speaker, or a brunch at the new kosher Chinese restaurant are some ideas which are fun and informative. A whole itinerary may be planned for "a day in Jewish Philadelphia/New York/our town" which outlines points of Jewish interest in one's city. This may include tracing the history of the Jews in the community and visiting those sections.

The havurah may want to attend a conference in another city or spend a weekend at the B'nai B'rith educational institutes (or something of a similar nature) or with the Lubavitcher Hasidim in Brooklyn. A wonderful experience is having a *Shabbaton* at a camp or at a secluded lodge or inn for an entire weekend. A camping trip is also something which can be quite appropriate during Sukkot or Shavuot.

Other Types of Meetings

If the havurah is family-oriented, the adults may want to get together for an "adult dinner" for a change of pace. Of course, there are the "planning meetings," which have been described above.

One of the most rewarding types of meetings in a havurah is the planning and sharing of a life cycle event of the members. A bar/bat mitzvah is a wonderful way of not only sharing in the *simhah* of the youngster, but also of having a role in the preparation. The members can contribute in terms of preparing the food and part (or all) of the service, providing resources during the youngster's study of his/her Torah and Haftarah portions, and possibly teaching him/her the *trup*.

The youngster may also opt to replace the traditional "thank you" speech with what is known as a creative bar/bat mitzvah project. This requires the youngster to choose an area of interest to him/her which relates to Jewish life (such as Soviet Jewry, the role of the Jewish woman throughout Jewish history, synagogue architecture, etc.). He/she is to research the topic over a year's time and prepare a presentation of it at his/her bar/bat mitzvah. The presentation can be in the form of a talk (with posters), a slide presentation, a model of his/her topic, or some other way that can tap the creativity of the youngster. This sense of responsibility is supported not only by his/her parents (who are the primary tutors, if possible) but also by the members of the group.

Another kind of meeting which challenges the group's adaptability is when there are pressing or immediate issues, such as personality problems which hinder the functioning of the group as a whole, a death or other tragic events, or some other emergency. A meeting of this type can also be held for happy events, such as a surprise birthday party, an anniversary celebration, or some other *simhah*.

RESULTS

Group Personality

The different types of meetings and activities described above provide a wide array of experiences which the members of a havurah can share with each other. Various patterns of responses begin to emerge and take shape as the group develops. This "group personality" often affects the nature and frequency of certain kinds of meetings. For example, there may be a tendency to schedule more social and/or cultural events than religious functions, or the group may prefer dealing with community-wide issues, such as Soviet Jewry or anti-Semitism, within the context of a havurah meeting, rather than by attendance at rallies or demonstrations. Another example of the way in which the group personality manifests itself is around certain proclivities, such as food. A havurah may "love to eat" and therefore may plan a number of functions which include meals as part of the get-together.

Effective Feedback

In the beginning of the group's development, the members may evaluate certain activities and/or meetings regarding the content, format, degree of involvement, etc. Time could be set aside toward the end of the meeting for such a discussion. As the members feel comfortable with each other and a sense of trust is established, feedback on a more personal level (misunderstandings, personality clashes) is to be encouraged. Whether an issue is to be raised with the entire group or just with those directly involved depends on the nature of the problem and how widespread it is among the members. In either case, such gatherings should be in a supportive environment—one in which a person may be critical of another's behavior without necessarily rejecting the individual.

As feedback (on both a personal and an activity level) becomes more a part of the group's functioning, such sessions can be scheduled on a more informal basis. Also, there are periods in the Jewish calendar which lend themselves to self-examination. The High Holy Days would be a time to reflect upon various aspects of the group. As long as feedback is an integral element of the havurah, the members can be more aware of changes taking place (or not taking place) and can plan for ways to adapt and grow.

A Sense of Community

One of the purposes of a havurah is to help fill a void in our society – the need to be part of a caring and trusting group of people outside of (or in addition to) one's immediate family. In many respects, a havurah is quite similar to an extended family. While no one is expected to be "best friends" with the members of his/her group, there is often a feeling of closeness. There is also an implicit acceptance of each person, including both the strengths and weaknesses of the individual.

This kind of base allows the havurah to move beyond the stated topics and activities into areas which may touch upon the personal lives of the members. This is not to say that the havurah is to be everyone's "big brother" or a therapy group. But it can be a focal point, a fulcrum upon which one can attempt to find some balance in his/her life. For example, during periods of emotional upheaval, one may find security and stability in the havurah. Financial straits may produce a helping hand from the group in terms of actual cash assistance. A visit to an ailing member in the hospital or helping someone pack and move are other ways of touching the lives of the members. It is this fusing of the social, cultural, and religious aspects of the havurah that transforms such a group into an organic community – one that responds to the needs of its members and, in its own way, helps give meaning to their lives.

CONCLUSION

A havurah is not for the person who is looking for minimal participation. It is not for the individual who does not compromise. It is intended to produce sweat and tears at times, because people's emotions are invested. These emotions are stretched and intertwined in an effort to broaden and deepen the lives of those involved in such a venture. Forming a havurah is a venture with few precedents, few boundaries, and few limitations to the creative and spiritual potentials of a group. It may not, as was stated in the beginning of this paper, be an elixir for our disjointed community. However, it may provide the challenge with which to begin to put the pieces together.

Israel

■ ■ ■ A Brief Introduction

The existence of the State of Israel provides the Jewish educator with enormous challenges. Some of them are somewhat paradoxical. On the one hand, the continued existence of a Jewish state is an absolute imperative of modern Jewish life. The Jewish educator thus feels the responsibility for developing a deep and abiding loyalty to Israel on the part of his or her students. The very urgency of the task, however, can often lead to simplistic and unsophisticated approaches to securing the loyalty of Jewish students. Particularly from a Reconstructionist point of view, the goal of our teaching efforts must be to help students become thinking Zionists.

The following two articles are presented with that aim in mind. The contribution of Meir Ben-Horin seeks to elucidate, in the broadest possible terms, the effects of Israel's existence on all dimensions of a Jewish education program. If Ben-Horin (following the lead of Ben-Gurion, whose six theses he expands) is correct, then the existence of Israel serves to normalize Jewish existence and thus demands a naturalistic approach to areas of the curriculum which previously could be taught in a supernatural vein. The second article, a simulation of the Sixth Zionist Congress, was developed by the staff of the Ann Spak Thal School of Society Hill Synagogue. It was designed to introduce elementary and junior high school students to the variety and textures of Zionist thought, to highlight the value of *ahavat Yisrael*, and to place the modern efforts to resettle Eretz Yisrael in a historical perspective.

Six Theses
on Jewish Education*

■ ■ ■ Meir Ben-Horin

Students of current Jewish affairs have paid far too little attention to one of the very significant pronouncements on the meaning of Israel's rebirth made since the Declaration of Independence of the Jewish State.

David Ben-Gurion, prime minister of Israel, in his address on May 25, 1952 before the Convocation of the Jewish Theological Seminary of America, whose president had come to Jerusalem to confer upon him the honorary degree of Doctor of Hebrew Letters, issued what may come to be regarded as a preamble to the Declaration of Independence of the Jewish Mind.

Delivered by the head of the Jewish State's first government, this pronouncement may, in the future, be taken as an authoritative summation of the thoughts, aspirations, and ideals cherished by the responsible Jewish political and intellectual leaders of our time. Yet no matter what its significance for the thinkers and scholars of coming generations, we of the second half of the twentieth century ought to ponder it, criticize it, defend or reject it—and certainly know it.

In the following paragraphs an effort is made, through the presentation of Ben-Gurion's main propositions[1] and the writer's educational

---

* This essay is reprinted, with the author's permission, from *Common Faith—Uncommon People* (New York: Reconstructionist Press, 1970).
1. All quotations are from the translation of the prime minister's address appearing in *Israel Digest* 2 (June 20, 1952).

theses derived therefrom, to formulate some of the statement's implications for Jewish education in our time. This is done on the assumption, first, that education, as the primary agency of social and individual improvement, dare not be found lagging in vision and resigning itself to the expediency of mere conventionality; second, that education, in order to function as an enlightening force in Jewish life, must reckon with the climate of opinion prevailing on the intellectual and social frontiers of the society in which it serves; and third, that education, in order to act as a guiding force in Jewish life, must adopt an affirmative orientation toward the home-building or Zion-building possibilities of Jewish civilization.

PROPOSITION ONE

With the birth of the State, a fundamental change has come about in the way we see ourselves and the world and in the way the world sees us. Our inner and outer nature is being fashioned anew. We are drawing ever closer to the source and historic root of our nationhood and to the spiritual legacy of the Biblical period. At the same time we are increasingly becoming free citizens of the great world, more and more integrated into the universal human heritage shared by all generations and all peoples.

Educational Thesis

The ideal personality to be envisaged by Jewish education, serving to give focus to its choices and direction to its processes, ought to be the informed, the intelligent, and the faithful Jew: informed of the needs, the failures, the accomplishments of the human race; intelligent in choosing among the institutions, the methods, and the principles evolved by the associations of men in the course of history; faithful to the supreme value of individual personality, socialized through participation in national culture, and humanized through integration in "the universal human heritage shared by all generations and peoples." This ideal of what, for want of a better term, may be called *the educated Jew* supersedes such Second Exile ideals as, for example, the Master of Talmudic Law and Logic; the Pious Follower of the Codes on Belief and Observance; the Martyr; the Silent Sufferer; the Mystic Dreamer; and, more recently, the Labor Pioneer; the Hero of the Underground; the Chief-of-Staff in Israel's Defense Forces. The new ideal, while reflecting the priceless idealism of Jewish generations steadfastly advancing through the Second Exile, is expressive of Jewry's newly-won confidence in its own humanity and in the humanity of its neighbors. It is evidence of Jewry's old-new sense of oneness at the same time with the human race and with its own far-flung congregations. That it could be expressed by the Prime Minister of Israel only seven years after the great Catastrophe in Central Europe is proof of the fact that irrepressibly the sap of life rises once again to the crown of the Tree of Life that is Israel's ancient and modern culture.

PROPOSITION TWO

> The passing of time has affected us, as it affects all nations, and no modern nation can or should be what it was a thousand or two or three thousand years ago. The revival of Israel's independence does not mean revival, in unaltered and unbending form, of our past. On the contrary, Israel's face is turned to the future. But that future is nourished by the source of our national vitality and absorbs into itself all the radiance of our past. For the past lives in us, not we in the past.

Educational Thesis

Jewish education must become reality- and future-centered. Modern Jewish schools, colleges, universities, must not be patterned after the image of their forebears in, say, Babylonia, Spain, medieval Germany, Russia, and Poland. Their primary mission must be to function as centers in which there go forward the reinterpretation of Jewish values, the study of the reorganization of Jewish communities, the reactivation of Jewish collective and individual creativity, the fashioning of the educated Jew as citizen-builder of modern Jewish society, the reconstruction of Jewish civilization.[2]

PROPOSITION THREE

> Rabbi Johanan ben Zakai, who asked the Roman conqueror for the boon of Yavneh and its wise men, may well have preserved Israel's existence and fortified its spirit against the misfortunes and sorrows it was to encounter during its prolonged wanderings. But the greatest among the disciples of Rabbi Johanan ben Zakai's disciples—Rabbi Akiba, son of Joseph, the outstanding figure in Judaism after the second destruction—was not satisfied merely with the existence of

---

2. Cf. my "Some Implications for Jewish Educational Institutions of Jewish Studies in American Institutions" in *The Education of American Jewish Teachers*, Oscar I. Janowsky, ed. (Boston: Beacon Press, 1967), pp. 272 ff.

Yavneh and its wise men, but aided Bar-Kokhba in the revolt intended to restore Israel's political sovereignty and freedom. It was only after the failure of that desperate and heroic attempt that the Jews became "the people of the Book," endeavoring to make commentaries on the Bible, and commentaries on those commentaries fill the gap left by the destruction of their sovereignty and of that rounded, full life which is enjoyed only by an independent nation. The Book that had come into being out of a historic background of freedom, in a fatherland related to the countries surrounding it, could no longer be understood in its genuine and original sense by the Jewish people.

Educational Thesis

Jewish education must become experience-centered rather than book-centered. The State of Israel signifies not only Jewry's return to the soil, but, more importantly, the Jewish people's resumption of direct relations with primary experience, with the "stuff of life" itself. Back in 1895 in tsarist Russia, Ahad Ha-Am, philosopher of cultural Zionism, had deplored the status of Jews as "the People of the Book" rather than "the People of Literature." Distinguishing between the fixity of the Book and the dynamic quality of a literature that is responsive to the flux of reality, he had sought to revitalize Jewish culture by advocating an education and a literature which would unite the stream of Jewish life with the broader stream of life in general without thereby losing its identity. Today, both long- and short-term needs in the State of Israel and in Western democratic society urgently demand the reapplication of Jewish creative energy not to literature but to the massive ore of experience itself. In Israel, a new sociopolitical structure, free from exploitation and oppressive government, must rise from millennial oscillation between timidity and temerity, flight into cosmic speculation and meticulous attention to the minutiae of ritual, selfless Utopianism and rugged opportunism, assimilation and isolation, petrifying fear of annihilation and breathless panting for the messiah. In the free Diaspora, new forms of community organization need to be invented and designed to cope with the novel challenge, inherent in a democratic order, to traditional Jewish institutions, which are themselves striving to achieve internal democracy. Jewish education no longer can afford to indulge in the ornamental luxury of mere "learning." Jewish schools must become the workshop and the laboratory for generations of young Jews eager to learn how to face up to primary experience with the resources of the Jewish people's culture.

PROPOSITION FOUR

It has now become impossible to deny that we continued to be a people during the entire period of our exile. It is true that we were—

and are, and will be—a unique people, a people *sui generis*. We preserved our distinctive character through the ages, and we will preserve it in the future. Yet, when our ancestors divided the world into two groups, Jews and Gentiles, they somewhat naively exaggerated the similarity among all people but themselves. In all probability every people considers itself unique—and rightly so. It is only in the degree, the extent and the significance of their distinctiveness that peoples differ.

Educational Thesis

Jewish education must seek to develop a conception of Jewish uniqueness that lays no claim to Jewish moral or religious superiority or *chosenness*, for there is nothing unique about such a claim. Loyalty to Judaism ought to flow from the experience of Jewish community life, from the concreteness of Jewish society, from the indispensable services rendered and required by Jewish peoplehood. As the civilization of the Jewish people, Judaism is valuable *per se*, just as human personality and as other civilizations are valuable *per se*. Jewish education now ought to become serious about the interdependence of individuals, groups, nations, and cultures in the modern world, all intrinsically valuable. It ought to stand guard alike against the decadent tendencies toward national self-obliteration, and against the importunities of national arrogance and self-adoration. Jewish education must build our inner defenses against anti-Semitism and at the same time it must expand our intercommunication system with democratic mankind. It must help us to become organic with the world.

In Ben-Gurion's words: "As free men we can—and, indeed, we must—see ourselves in the past and in the present, as we are, with all our faults and inadequacies and defects. Instead of pointing out our good sides to others, we will endeavor to develop our blessed heritage and to inculcate in ourselves all the positive human qualities, for we are part of humanity and nothing human is alien to us. We shape our lives and our culture in loyalty to the great light of our past, participating to the fullest extent possible in the fundamental, all-human values developed by the great thinkers and teachers of our day."

PROPOSITION FIVE

Research and scholarship in the State of Israel must now embrace the whole world—the study of atoms and stars, plants and animals, the hidden resources of the earth and the seas, winds and weather and all the mysteries of nature in the heavens above and the ground below;

the chronicles of man from the time he appeared on the scene of life, his struggles, his achievements and his failures, his strife with himself and his fellows, in private and in public, in all periods and all lands. All these are the subjects with which scholars in Israel will have to concern themselves. So, too, literature in Israel will have to include not only books written originally in Hebrew and books in other languages by Jews or about Judaism, but all the treasures of the human spirit from antiquity to the present – the ancient writings of Egypt, Babylon, China, India, Persia, Arabia, Greece and Rome; the heritage of the Middle Ages and modern times in the fields of science, art, philosophy, religion and poetry.

Educational Thesis

Education in the State of Israel ought to join hands with Jewish education throughout the world in a combined effort to formulate and to cast into an educational mold a new synthesis of world culture and Jewish culture. No intellectual problem needs to be more carefully explored by Jewish youth in our time than that posed by the impact of science and democracy on Jewish nationalism and religion, on the one hand, and the potential impact of Jewish civilization on the morality of science and democracy on the other. Hence, no educational program should be considered adequate that fails to address itself to this problem and to guide students toward a better grasp of the issues involved. No elementary school, high school or college established for the purpose of fostering and advancing Jewish culture discharges its obligation toward the evolving Jewish civilization when it fails to help the maturing minds of our young to become intelligent about the most serious challenge that traditional Judaism ever encountered in history. It is now the primary duty of Jewish education to integrate Jewish and scientific-democratic values so that once again Judaism may come to be regarded by our people not merely as a matter of conspicuous respectability and filial piety, but as an intellectual force to be reckoned with in the market place, the stock exchange, and the santuary of ideas.

PROPOSITION SIX

[We need] utter freedom of thought, independence of spirit, lack of prejudice and of defensive or offensive intentions.... The search for truth suffers no chains and no bounds. The spirit of our people in exile was chained, and only with the revival of our independence has it been freed from the internal and external restraints which narrowed, limited and distorted its activities.

Educational Thesis

Jewish education in the Diaspora, lest it become alienated from what Ben-Gurion calls "the new wisdom of Israel," must emancipate itself and the young generations in its trust from the perennial confusion of myth and history, of poetry and verified fact, of hypothesis and secured knowledge, of time-bound assumptions and the time-tested foundations of socio-religious idealism. Neither science nor democracy must remain the exclusive domain of extra-Jewish education. The faith in man and the ideal of life abundant inherent in both must animate educational effort in a free society, Jewish or non-Jewish. Expressed in terms of liberal strands in the Hebraic tradition and reinforced by their *partiality toward the disinterested pursuit of truth,* [3] this faith and this ideal must vibrate through the "continuous reconstruction of Jewish experience" which is Jewish education.

---

3. "...disinterestedness is the keynote of the best scientific efforts.... You understand, entire surrender of self: that is what I call disinterestedness; nothing less. One cannot help feeling that any such disinterested effort must increase the sum of good will in the world." From George Sarton, *The History of Science and the New Humanism* (Bloomington: Indiana University Press, 1962), pp. 116, 117.

A Simulation of the Sixth Zionist Congress

■ ■ ■ Staff of
Society Hill Synagogue's
Ann Spak Thal School

Few events in the history of modern Zionism evoked such passion as the so-called Uganda proposal. The proposal was initiated by the British government in 1902. It offered an African homeland to the Jewish people. The proposal was misnamed; the territory being offered was in East Africa, in the territory of present-day Kenya. Historians often make the mistake of treating the issue as if the fate of the Uganda proposal was determined by the Zionist response to it. Ultimately, the proposal was scrapped because the European colonialists in East Africa were not eager to share the wealth of their land with "poor Russian Jews," and they waged an effective campaign against the proposal within the British Foreign Office.

The popular understanding of the Uganda plan as a test case for the intensity of Jewish feeling about Eretz Yisrael, however, is essentially correct. It is important to understand just how great a role *emotion* played in the debate. The division at the Sixth Zionist Congress was not between those who accepted Jewish nationalism and those who did not. All who were present accepted Jewish nationalism in one form or another. The division was not between the "political" Zionists of Western Europe and the "practical" Zionists of Eastern Europe. (Sachar points out how advocacy crossed these so-called party lines.) Nor was the division really between those who favored Palestine as a Jewish homeland and those who did not. Most of the supporters of the Uganda proposal saw it as a diplomatic bridgehead to an eventual Jewish settlement in Palestine. The real division was between those for whom *ahavat Zion* — love of Zion — was ingrained at such an emotional level that they could not consider a pragmatic alternative to a Jewish homeland in Palestine, and those whose love of Israel — while no less authentic — was less visceral and who could consider such a possibility.

Suggested Background Reading for Teachers:

Howard Sachar, *A History of Israel* (Jewish Publication Society), pp. 59-63. Robert Weisbord, *African Zion* (Jewish Publication Society).

Objectives of Simulation

The basic goal of this simulation is to help students to experience the intense emotional attachment of Jews to the land of Israel and the ideological conflict that occurred when the material welfare of the Jewish people seemed to dictate a temporary abandonment of Palestine as the Jewish homeland. A secondary goal, most appropriate for high school students, is to be able to use this simulation as a springboard for understanding the complex history and ideology of modern Zionism. We have used this simulation effectively, as described in the "Basic Format" section following, for a group of ten- to twelve-year-olds in a forty-five minute assembly. The suggestions in the "Variations" section are ways of expanding the scope and depth of the simulation.

Basic Format

1. **Establishing Setting**. The class is constituted as the Sixth Zionist Congress. (A banner reading "Sixth World Zionist Congress, Welcome to Basel, Switzerland" helps establish the setting.) The congress is informed that they have a crucial decision to make that will affect the course of Jewish history. They are read the following message of the Zionist movement. It should be delivered with great feeling and exaggerated dignity (both typical of Herzl).

> Fellow Jews,
>   Our efforts to establish a homeland for the Jewish people have come to a sharp turning point. I regret to inform you that my contacts with the Turkish authorities have not proved fruitful. The Sultan will not grant us a charter to settle Palestine as we wish, no matter what I offer him in return. Nor has our second line of attack proved effective. As you know, our feeling has been that if we cannot receive a charter for the historic Jewish homeland of Palestine from Turkish

authorities, perhaps we can persuade the British authorities to give us the right of settlement in El Arish in the Sinai. This would put us in direct proximity [show map if available] to Eretz Yisrael and would also give us title to historic Jewish land, the land where Moses and the children of Israel wandered in the wilderness.

Gentlemen, it pains me greatly to report this lack of progress to you. As you know, our people are being violently assaulted in Russia. Spilled Jewish blood cries out from Russia for us to do something...and to do something now. I have just visited Russia and cannot tell you how great is the suffering there.

There is an alternative. It is not what we had hoped for, but it may yet be a step in the direction of our most cherished dream. I have in mind a memorandum from Mr. Leopold Greenberg informing us that the government of Great Britain would be willing to support a Jewish colony in some of the territory it holds in Africa. Gentlemen, in view of the grave condition of our fellow Jews in Russia, I suggest that we accept the British government's offer. We shall never abandon our dreams of Palestine. But an African homeland will provide refuge for the night.

2. **Work Groups**. The Zionist Congress is divided into three groups. Approximately one half of the group should remain as voting delegates. The remaining half is divided between the pro-Uganda and anti-Uganda groups. Their job is to present as persuasive a case as possible for or against the proposal. For approximately half an hour, participants work in their respective groups on the following tasks.

Delegates. This group must come to understand what some of the underlying issues are, so as to make the right decision. They have the responsibility of being a "vital center" that can and will be more reasonable than the pro or anti forces. The delegates should answer the following questions in writing individually and then share their answers in small groups.

a. Here are some of the things at stake in the Uganda proposal. Put them in the order of their importance for the Jewish people.

Freedom from physical danger for the Jewish people _____
Working and living in the land where Hebrew was originally spoken and where the Bible developed _____
A country that will allow Jews to become productive farmers and provide a living for themselves _____
Living in peace with the non-Jews in the country you will settle _____
Living in the Jewish people's historic homeland _____

b. Most of the delegates to the congress know very little about Uganda. Make a list of questions you would like answered about this little-known territory that will help you know whether it is a suitable homeland for Jews.

c.   From Herzl's talk and your own (as yet) uninformed ideas about the Uganda proposal, make a list of all the pros and cons you can think of about the proposal.

d.   Go back to a. Will Uganda or Palestine most help you achieve your number one value? Why?

Pro-Uganda. Two activities. One group is given a list of some of the arguments in favor of the Uganda proposal. They may add their own. This group must decide which of the arguments are most persuasive, how the arguments can best be presented, and who should present them. The list of pro-Uganda arguments would include:

a.   Uganda can help the Jews now when they need it. Palestine is still a dream.

b.   The soil of Uganda is much better suited to agriculture than Palestine. The climate is better suited to Europeans than is Palestine.

c.   The fact that Britain is offering the colony is important. It means that one of the world's major powers is saying that Zionism is good and legitimate. This will give Jews a lot more prestige in the eyes of non-Jews.

d.   Uganda now does not mean that Palestine couldn't come later. In fact, having a Jewish colony in Africa might convince the Turks that the Jews can govern their own country.

e.   When Jews were allowed to run their own affairs and were not discriminated against by ruling governments, they were able to live fairly well outside of Israel. Being outside of Israel (Palestine) isn't automatically bad for the Jews.

f.   Herzl's very address shows how difficult the Turkish government which controls Palestine can be. It's better to take an offer from the British. It will mean more because Britain is stronger and will keep its word.

The other group should work on some posters that can be displayed while the pro-Uganda side is arguing. Sayings like "Jews Need a Homeland NOW" and "You Can't Say No to the World's Greatest Power" would be appropriate. A more talented student might want to try something like a satirical cartoon captioned with "Only Palestine Will Satisfy Us" and a picture of a pogrom in the background.

Anti-Uganda. The same two basic activities go on here. Some of the possible anti-Uganda arguments are:

a.   There are Jewish settlers already in Palestine. There are no such settlers in Uganda.

b.   Jews are emotionally attached to Palestine. They have prayed to return to it for two thousand years. They will work much harder to create a Jewish state in Palestine than anywhere else.

c. While Herzl may not be able to get a charter from the Turkish government, there is a different way to build a Jewish settlement: to do it acre by acre, from the beginning. This doesn't seem as dramatic, but it's the best way in the long run to create a Jewish state.

d. There's no guarantee that Britain will be able to keep her word about a colony for Jews.

e. A homeland in Africa would be farther removed from Europe than one in Palestine. It would be less able to be part of the events affecting Jews in Europe.

The second group would also work on posters for when the anti-Uganda presentation is made. Some possibilities are posters that read, "At the Pesah Seder We Read 'Next Year in Jerusalem'—not 'Next Year in Africa'" or "Tell *King* Herzl that the Jewish People Want Palestine." Another poster might have a map of Africa with a big X over the area of East Africa with NO in bright letters at the bottom. On the other side of the poster would be a map of Palestine with a big YES marked under it.

3. **Debate.** Each side presents its case for five minutes. After five minutes of rebuttal time for each faction, the debate is thrown open to the delegates.

4. **Vote.** Three possible courses of action are debated and then voted upon. The one with the most votes (only delegates vote) is the action adopted by the Sixth World Zionist Congress.

Accept the proposal outright.

Reject the proposal outright.

Send a commission of inquiry to Uganda to report back to the next Zionist Congress.

5. **Process.** Help the participants get a better understanding of the simulation by asking questions such as: "At what point did you feel most involved in the simulation?" "Was there one particular argument that was most persuasive for you?" "What might things be like today if Zionists had accepted the Uganda plan? Would it have affected the Holocaust in any way?" "Which side seemed to rely most on reason? Which on emotion?" "Do you think *ahavat Zion*, love of Israel, meant something different for the Jews at the Sixth Zionist Congress than it does for you today?"

It's also important to give students some sort of factual follow-up on what actually happened at the Sixth World Congress. The course the congress eventually followed was to send a commission of inquiry to Africa. By this time, however, the resistance of European settlers who were already in East Africa had stiffened. Typically, Britain had no consistent colonial policy other than appeasing the group that it cared most about at a given moment. Meanwhile, the Second Aliyah began in Palestine and rooted Jews more firmly in Eretz Yisrael. By 1906, the whole raging issue had become irrelevant.

Variations

Teachers who would like to develop the simulation further might consider the following possibilities:

1. Expanding the depth of knowledge brought to the debate by making the simulation the culmination of a course in Zionism rather than an isolated special assembly.

2. Adding dramatic flourish by: (a) having key figures costumed as Herzl, Nordau, Ussishkin, etc.; (b) having the anti-Uganda group learn and sing *Hatikvah* as part of their presentation.

3. Adding Hebraic flavor by having groups research appropriate quotes from the *Tanakh* that either support or do not support the centrality of Eretz Yisrael for the Jewish people.

4. Adding emotional fervor by: (a) having demonstrations of approval and/or disapproval during debate; (b) encouraging students to make their points through symbolic statements. Rather than just talk about the Russian Jews slaughtered in the pogrom, have the pro-Uganda presenter read a letter from a Russian orphan, or have the anti-Uganda group make a papier-mâché arm with the quote in Hebrew and English, "If I forget thee, O Jerusalem, may my right hand lose its cunning."

5. Adding broad historical context by bringing in the perspective of non-Zionist Jewish opinion and non-Jewish opinion. This can be done by reading newspaper clippings at various times during the congress to give the participants a feeling for how the outside Jewish and non-Jewish world is viewing their actions or by adding demonstrators who burst into the congress to make their non-Zionist or anti-Semitic views known.

6. Adding contemporary relevance by discussing such issues as whether world Jewry could survive today without a Jewish homeland in Eretz Yisrael.

Educational Implications
of Reconstructionism*

■ ■ ■ Etan Levine

Over half a century ago, Professor Mordecai M. Kaplan defined and described Judaism as an evolving religious civilization. Fifty years later, the Reconstructionist "cultural revolution" he initiated still continues, and one of the arenas which has been most enriched is that of Jewish education in all of its forms. The civilizational approach to Judaism has profound educational consequences, not the least being that every Jew is both a teacher and a student of that civilization. The purpose of this brief essay is to touch upon the educational implications of Reconstructionist Judaism.

Primacy of Education

Human civilization consists of each generation's transmitting to successive generations its own accumulated record of experiences, emotions, and discoveries. Thus, education is actually the life process of society, with teaching and learning constituting its essential, organic function.

That which applies to civilization universally applies also to Jewish civilization. The future of Judaism as a creative, live option with a culturally pluralistic society will be determined largely by the success or failure of its educational structures and processes. Thus, aside from the intrinsic worth of its content, Jewish education is the primary medium for the survival, continuity, evolution, growth and revival of Judaism as a religious civilization. Reconstructionist Judaism is, *by definition*, a commitment to effective Jewish education. Further, it implies a series of commitments

---

* Reprinted from *Reconstructionist*, March, 1980.

as to the nature of Jewish education. The basic aspects of a Reconstructionist approach to Jewish education are worth consideration.

Telling Versus Teaching

There are numerous complicated and interrelated reasons for the inadequate effectiveness of contemporary Jewish education. However, most problems derive from the pedagogic inability or doctrinal reluctance to distinguish between "telling" and "teaching." Stated briefly, "telling" is the function of a book, oracle, guru, or information-storage-retrieval device. The traditional "telling" approach presupposes that learning consists of accumulating data, in a squirrel-like mode. "Teaching," on the other hand, consists of enabling students to internalize and react to assumedly-significant data, attitudes, and experiences. Reconstructionist education is, by definition, committed to "teaching" in the most honest sense.

A genuinely Reconstructionist approach to Jewish education requires a unique process. It involves an interpersonal exchange between the teachers and the taught, relating to the most profoundly personal dimensions of the participants themselves, and of human life itself. For Reconstructionist Judaism deals in ultimates and absolutes, as well as in immediate and relative values, ideas and experiences. In a very real sense, both the individual and the collective past, present, and future must be involved in the process. In "religious education" worthy of the name, the dimension of personal significance is infinite. It calls for in-depth teaching, not simply telling.

Three Dimensions

When Judaism is regarded as an evolving religious civilization, it is necessary to address three dimensions. These are the: a. Intellectual, b. Emotional, c. Behavioral. This division implies that religious education must be arranged along tripartite lines eventuating in: a. Knowledge, b. Sensitivity, c. Action. Stated alternatively, Jewish education must produce a given yield of a. Information, b. Commitment, c. Performance.

Although it is certainly legitimate to assign various levels of importance to each of these three dimensions, it is imperative to address all three of them, if one claims to be educating a whole human being. There is a necessary interrelation among these three elements: they are mutually supportive, not mutually exclusive.

Ideally, therefore, a Reconstructionist religious education consists of exposure to a coherent program providing the experiences of: a. Discovering, b. Emoting, and c. Doing. Obviously, the content of each dimension will perforce differ according to the specificity of the religious definitions and operational goals; but the three dimensions themselves will, of necessity, serve as the essential rubrics of the Reconstructionist educational structure.

Closed Versus Open Approaches

Consciously or otherwise, an initial determination is made by every educator: to what extent does he want to educate for closedness, and to what extent does he want to educate for openness? In other words, does he define his function as primarily one of indoctrination, or as essentially one of investigation? Alternatively stated, is his basic function the providing of predetermined answers, or is his primary role the raising of questions? The implications of this basic determination affect not only "style," but the content and scope of educational material; determining the type of terrain over which the educator is willing to tread, as well as his gait.

Reconstructionist Jewish education recognizes that, to the extent that the teacher enters into the educative relationship with preconceived notions of what "the answers" are, to that extent is the process "indoctrination." Investigation is punctuated by a question mark, not an exclamation point. Authentic Reconstructionist education involves the exploration of hypotheses; the sharing of thesis, antithesis, and synthesis. It is an adventure in discovery, in sharing and in creating.

Additionally, a Reconstructionist approach implies that all "answers" are tentative, and that the very idea of unchanging methods, ideas, and responses within a universal context of eternal change constitutes an absurdity.

The Teacher

There are numerous qualities with which a Reconstructionist educator is endowed. However, in identifying the Reconstructionist teacher, the two qualities which are absolutely essential are: a) he must himself be committed to the religious approach, he is teaching, and committed to the teaching of that religious approach; b) he must himself be involved in some religious growth experience.

Reconstructionist education consists of not simply teaching *about* religion, but of teaching religion *itself*. For an educator to convey that which does not infuse, excite, and involve him, and constitute an essential dimension of his very existence, is an impossibility. Even the attempt represents a sham.

One of the most debilitating experiences of the student is the discovery that his teacher has misrepresented the depth of his own religious commitment. A religious educator must, by definition, genuinely affirm his personal involvement with and commitment to the Jewish experience.

Similarly, to remain "alive," the Reconstructionist educator must be more than a liberal duplicate of the Orthodox educator. That is to say, he must be involved in growth experiences *himself*. He cannot aid the growth process of others unless he himself is experiencing the process. Using a very simple but telling index: Is he more today than he was yesterday? He may know very little, but if he knows more today than he knew yesterday, he is "alive." On the other hand, he may know very much, but if he knows no more today than he knew yesterday, he is "fossilized," and has lost his spiritual life process of growth, refinement, synthesis, response, self-correction, and development. One of the most uninspiring stereotypes within Jewish education is the uninspired educator who dispassionately dispenses the warmed-over truths he picked up yesterday.

Four Functions

Although there are numerous legitimate didactic methods which the religious educator adopts, a Reconstructionist approach includes four functions of the "complete" educator. These are: a) presenting a point of view, b) interpreting life experience, c) initiating experiences, d) eliciting criticism.

First, the Reconstructionist educator presents himself as a living contact. He is an accessible model to whom his students may react. He is a representative, an advocate and a case in point. He is a "witness," a member, and an authentic representative of the tradition he teaches. By representing a point of view, he brings the reality of his commitments, experiences, and knowledge into the orbit of his students.

Second, he interprets, organizes and integrates the cycle of experience to which his students are exposed. Thus, if Judaism is seen as a crucial fulcrum or vital center of human existence, it is the function of the religious educator to help his students organize, conceptualize, and positively relate to life in its parts and *in toto*. He provides a means of discovering and defining the guideposts, verities, stabilities, and inner resources that enable a person to live a human life in the Jewish idiom.

Third, the Reconstructionist educator structures experiences: confrontations with Jewish texts, people, ideas, and institutions, so that students may emerge from these experiences somehow enriched, enlarged, and enlightened. He is, therefore, a programmer of significant experiences, creating a curriculum of personal growth and development. In this function, he translates Jewish civilization from the theoretical into the actual.

The fourth function of the Reconstructionist educator is to elicit constructive criticism and purposeful change. Unless the educator vainly conceives of himself as an omniscient repository of eternal verities perfectly formulated, he will involve his students, as an expression of religious commitment, in the on-going task of refreshing and rejuvenating the religious heritage and religious expression.

One of the major obstacles to institutional Judaism today is the popular attitude (which is largely historically justified) that the religious establishment is defensive, rigid, and ossified. Today the educational challenge consists not of quashing the rebel, but of enlisting him; not of repressing but of involving the dissident. Unless our various Jewish institutions succeed in communicating a genuine interest in diversity, pluralism, and responsible opposition, they are simply dismissed out-of-hand as an arena for contemporary involvement. Reconstructionist education, therefore, welcomes dialogue; it shuns silence, not the arenas in which ideas compete for men's minds.

Means, Ends, and Cooperative Effort

Reconstructionist thought recognizes that all education is a process of transformation, a program for becoming. Needless to say, various religious orientations and various educational orientations within the Jewish community will differ radically as to the specific nature of the desired transformation. However, the Reconstructionist would argue that there need not be agreement as to desired ends, in order to effect sustained conversation and cooperation between Jewish educators of divergent orientations.

It is possible—and imperative—to study the appropriateness of specific educational means: whether a given situation calls for a given pedagogic response; what specific texts, curricula and procedures are efficiently, effectively related to desired goals; in short, what are the best means for producing the type of human being envisioned. Further, it is possible—and imperative—to discuss priorities, to evaluate the psycho-social implications of methodology, to analyze prevailing assertions. To a Reconstructionist, the Jewish community is itself capable of serving as a kind of learning laboratory; a crucible that actually exists in classrooms, homes, institutions, and houses of worship.

It may not be an exaggeration to say that the viability of the Jewish community will, to a large extent, be determined by the effectiveness of Jewish education. And success in Jewish education will be determined by the effectiveness of Jewish education. And success in Jewish education will be determined by the extent of cooperation and sharing of experience among concerned and skilled educators. It is inconceivable that there not be a forum of Reconstructionist-oriented educators bridging the continents, spanning elementary, secondary, and higher levels, including formal and informal education, and dedicated to participation in "the greater Judaism in the making."

Ethical and Folk Components
of Jewish Storytelling

■ ■ ■ Peninnah Schram

The Jewish People has always been the People of the Book and the Word. Therein lies the tale, for each one of us carries within himself an entire tribe with a complete cycle of legends, dances, and songs. Each person is made up of a million voices, tastes, smells, memories, and hopes. The Jew remembers all of this through his storytelling. Nathan Ausubel writes in *A Treasury of Jewish Folklore* (p. xvii):

> I was immersed in Jewish song and story as soon as I became aware of the world around me. Years later, I discovered that the lore of my people had entered into my blood stream, as it were, and had become a part of the cultural reality of my life. Who has not had this experience? Melodies sung in childhood and the stories and sayings we heard time and again from the lips of our parents are never really erased from our memory.

As one can see, storytelling is a shared experience whether in the home or in the synagogue; at the Seder or at the Megillah reading; sitting on the lap of one's parent or sitting on the *bimah*. Stories are what is passed from one generation to another.

This idea is contained in the poetic passage written by Elie Wiesel as a dedication to his *Souls on Fire*[1]:

---

1. Elie Wiesel, *Souls on Fire* (New York: Random House, 1972), 1.

My father, an enlightened spirit, believed in man. My grandfather, a fervent Hasid, believed in God. The one taught me to speak, the other to sing.

Both loved stories.

And when I tell mine, I hear their voices.

Whispering from beyond the silenced storm, they are what links the survivor to their memory.

Wiesel [2] also recalls how his grandfather told him to "listen attentively and above all, remember that true tales are meant to be transmitted—to keep them to oneself is to betray them." People, then, are the link between generations through stories.

There is a wealth of stories in our Jewish heritage, so let us begin with a story.

A long time ago there was a king who had a daughter. When the time came for the daughter to be married, the king decided to invite the entire kingdom to the celebration. The only gift he asked of his people was that they each bring a bottle of wine from their own vineyards. The king planned that everyone would pour his own bottle of wine into a huge vat. At the appropriate moment, each person would toast the bride and groom with a glass of wine from the vat—the wine that was a blend of everyone's contributions.

On the day of the wedding, the people came bringing the bottles of wine and poured them into the vat as they entered the palace gardens. When it was time to begin the toast, the king turned on the spigot for the first glass of wine. A strange thing happened. What came out was a clear liquid—water! It seems that each of the people in the kingdom thought: "Why should I bring my good wine? Why, if I bring a bottle of water, no one will ever know. With thousands of bottles of wine, my bottle will hardly dilute the rest of the wine so it won't make any difference." But everyone had had the same idea, and each brought only a bottle of water. Each person had made a difference.

I first heard this story told at a bar mitzvah ceremony. It instantly meant something to me—a deep note of recognition vibrated within me. The message clicked: what you put into a situation, you take out of it, and more. Since that time, I have not only retold this story on many occasions, but I have heard several other versions, including a Chelm version of this story. Where does the story come from? The person who had told it at the bar mitzvah told me she had found it in a magazine (she could not recall which one) and that the author had been "unknown."

---

2. *Ibid.*, 7.

Is the source originally midrashic or Hasidic? Or from another people? Who knows? That is what happens to a good story. It is told and adapted and told again. Sometimes we can find the source and other times we have to search further. I shall have to keep searching in this case.

I became fascinated with stories when I was very young. In fact, I don't remember a time without stories. With each story, I took a journey to visit distant lands (especially Israel), to meet new characters, to understand new ideas, to discover solutions and options, to take time to daydream, and particularly to internalize the values of Judaism and to feel part of the Jewish people. Through the verbal form of the story, I could experience the Jewish tradition in a powerful and elegant way. What was even more wonderful was that another person (my parent or teacher) was sharing this story with me. I was not alone. That person was giving me a gift. I felt important. I felt good. And I have not only remembered the stories, but have retold them to my children and to many other children.

The oral tradition was a part of my childhood. When my father indicated to us that he was going to tell me a story, something special happened to me. A whole imaginary world fused with my past, present, and future, along with what was and might have been. The magic words "I'm going to tell you a story" created an openness to listen and to know, to participate and to create. My father had invested a full measure of wine, sharing his knowledge, wisdom, values, and beliefs by telling me the stories of the Jewish people. In a real sense, we are all storytellers. It is through the telling that we can bring our true bottles of wine to share with our community of Jews.

This essay will have a two-fold purpose. It will deal first with how storytelling functions educationally for children, and second, with how Jewish education can utilize storytelling as a means for the transmission of values and the promotion of Jewish identity.

Education is not just the transmission of a collection of facts. It is helping another person to develop the ability to make connections. Education means a "drawing out" or "leading out." It is a reciprocal process between two people in which there is mutual contact and trust. As in all education, Jewish education is a continuous process which takes place in the home as well as in the school. However, it is in the home that the educational process has its greater impact. The education of a Jew is a process of ongoing exploration and reinterpretation. It is not a simple process, because the education should involve the study of history, language, folkways, and religion. Mordecai Kaplan identifies and discusses these four elements in his *Judaism as a Civilization*[3] and then focuses spe-

---

3. Mordecai M. Kaplan, *Judaism as a Civilization* (New York: Thomas Yoseloff, 1957), 186-202.

cifically on the "peoplehood" of the Jews as contributing primarily to our essential unity as Jews. The spotlight is always on the idea that people are of the highest import, and that all religious symbols, worship, prayer, rituals, and activities are only important in that they help to develop the sense of group unity in addition to group continuity. In this way, "a religion fortifies the collective consciousness."[4] Along with this "collective consciousness," the Jews have as their purpose the development of "a sense of moral responsibility in action."[5]

What is it that makes stories an effective medium for promoting group identity and values? Storytelling derives its power from several features. Let us consider three of these features.

Appeal to Senses

The first of these is the power of stories to evoke an appeal to the senses. Our Jewish tradition often makes use of the senses in order to teach as an experiential method. The havdalah ceremony is a good example of this. By including the sensory appeal within the stories, an immediacy and an involvement is created, not only in the actions, but also in the sense experience. We "taste" the fruits of Israel, we "smell" the fresh scent of morning dew, we "hear" the harp of David and his songs, we "see" the flames, we "touch" the Torah, we "feel" the pain and the joy of being Jewish, and more. Seeing, feeling, tasting, smelling, touching, hearing: all our senses, which help us to learn and to identify with our tradition, are stimulated through the spoken word.

In discussing the importance of the senses and ritual in Judaism, Kaplan contends that "Judaism is not merely a universe of discourse but also a universe of sense experience."[6] After all, it is through the senses that one recalls emotions. It is the emotions that cause one to act. This is not to say that we should toss away the reasoning component and the intellectual approach to Judaism. Not at all. What this does mean is that Judaism requires a holistic approach. Kaplan interprets it this way:[7]

> Creativity is the result of whole-souled and organic reaction to life's values; of a reaction in which senses, emotions, imagination, intelligence and will are fully aroused. It is not enough for a civilization to be rich in the values of a religious or aesthetic nature. Unless its people respond wholeheartedly to those values, the civilization is artistically sterile.

---

4. *Ibid.*, 333.
5. *Ibid.*, 318.
6. *Ibid.*, 435.
7. *Ibid.*, 485.

Indeed, the sensory recall and the sense experience combined with meaning are "the material of religio-poetic feeling"[8] within the person. This in turn creates "emotional identification with the inner life of a people, and as a means of expressing the feeling of life's significance in the individual manner of that people."[9] The focus, as we can see, is always on the people, the group, and the development of conscience and self-consciousness within that group or folk. As a consequence of developing this consciousness, Judaism as a folk religion serves "as a means of integrating the aspirations of the individual with the ideals of his community."[10]

Group Identity

The second feature of storytelling that plays a prominent role in educating and developing group identity and values is the open sharing of the folk experience through stories. Scholars in the field of communication have begun to discover that the oral transmission of tales are literally mind-expanding. In his article entitled "Paleoneurology and the Evolution of Mind," Harry Jerison states that "We need language more to tell stories than to direct actions."[11] He continues,

> In the telling we create mental images in our listeners that might normally be produced only by the memory of events as recorded and integrated by the sensory and perceptual systems of the brain.
>   Mental images should be as real, in a fundamental sense, as the immediately experienced real world. Both are constructions of the brain, although it is appropriate to encode them in order to distinguish image from reality. The role of language in human communication is special because we have the vocal and manual apparatus to create spoken and written language. In hearing or reading another's words we literally share another's consciousness, and it is that familiar use of language that is unique to man. The point, however, is that it was necessary to have a brain that created the kind of consciousness communicated by the motor mechanisms of language. That new capacity required an enormous amount of neural tissue, and much of the expansion of the human brain resulted from the development of language and related capacities for mental imagery.

---

8. *Ibid.*, 435.
9. *Ibid.*
10. *Ibid.*, 341.
11. Harry J. Jerison, "Paleoneurology and the Evolution of Mind," *Scientific American* 232 (January 1976):101.

While the brain of a young child develops to handle the mental imagery and language, the child needs to be fed the language and the mental imagery. In this way, storytelling serves to expand a child's horizons.

Storytelling, whether in the home or at work, at weddings, at wakes, or at other celebrations, is found everywhere. Stories traveled and were adapted to reflect the life experiences and values of each particular society. Some stories were adopted without much change. Because of this, there are similar themes, plots, and characters in almost every culture.

No one knows when folktales began—certainly long before there was a written language. However, many of the traveling merchants were Jews, and since Jews have always been a storytelling people, Jews played a key role in the transmission of folktales.

> The Jews may well be described as the great disseminators of folk-lore. Many a legend that originated in Egypt or Babylonia was appropriated by the European peoples, and many a European fairy tale found its way to Asia through the medium of the Jews who, on their long wanderings from the East to the West, and back from the West to the East, brought the products of oriental fancies to the occidental nations and the creations of the occidental imagination to the oriental peoples.[12]

In Europe, it was principally the Grimm brothers and Andersen who gathered and preserved the words of peasants or refashioned the folk-tales they heard by using dynamic and colorful language. They understood that the richness of language which captured the folk imagination fed the mental images and promoted mental growth.

In the early nineteenth century, before many children's books had appeared in England, Charles Lamb stressed that a child's power of imagination should be nurtured by fairy tales. He felt a child's sense of wonder could be satisfied only by a literature that had grown out of the same sense of wonder. These authors knew that stories could establish the connection between the child and the characteristics of the culture, the values, the folkways. In the opinion of folklorist Linda Degh, storytelling "is the vital link that provides the means for transmission of the folktale tradition."[13]

The telling of stories creates a common core of tradition and values which can be passed on to new generations. In many societies, including

---

12. Louis Ginzberg, *The Legends of the Jews* (Philadelphia: Jewish Publication Society of America, 1925), 5:vii.

13. Anne Pellowski, *The World of Storytelling* (New York: R. R. Bowker, 1977), 44.

those of the Xhosa and Zulu tribes, the ideas of the society are communicated by oral narratives in an aesthetically compelling fashion. In these societies everyone is a potential storyteller and thereby a teacher, "and each has the opportunity to analyze and comment upon his society through the system of narrative images."[14] In the Pueblo society, the child does not receive the command "Do this," but rather hears a tale "designed to explain how children first came to know that it was right to 'do this,' and detailing the sad results that befall those who did otherwise."[15] Again, we can see that storytelling is not a private experience, but a shared experience which involves language, mental imagery, and sensory recall, as well as cultural traditions and customs. Storytelling is transformed into a folk experience.

Beginning in the early eighteenth century, the Hasidim brought the oral tradition back to the folk experience in Jewish life. While the *tzadik*, or leader, first tells the tales to the people,

> The tales may grow imperceptibly as they pass among the people, each teller adding his words until the image is complete; or they may be made in entirety by one who is so completely within his folk as to speak with the voice of the entire people. The Chassidic legend is drawn from both these sources.[16]

What kind of tales did the Hasidim tell? Wonder tales of miraculous deeds performed by the rebbe; fairy tales of a king and a princess; mystical tales; simple tales and complex tales. With all the rich variety of their subject matter, all the stories contain the full scope of life: the love of God, the joyful approach to prayer and existence, the beliefs and values of the Hasidim.

In the Hasidic world today, the oral tradition remains a part of the religious and social life. Storytelling is shared in their synagogues, at Shabbos meals, on the anniversary of a famous rebbe's death, and whenever Hasidim come together to pray, dance, and sing.

There are many functions that the tales serve in Hasidic culture. Jerome R. Mintz, in his book *Legends of the Hasidim*, mentions two of these purposes:[17]

---

14. Harold Scheub, "Fixed and Nonfixed Symbols in Xhosa and Zulu Narrative Traditions," *Journal of American Folklore* 85:267.
15. Marie L. Shedlock, *The Art of the Storyteller* (New York: Dover, 1951), 102.
16. Meyer Levin, *Classic Hassidic Tales* (New York: The Citadel Press, 1966), xii.
17. Jerome R. Mintz, *Legends of the Hasidim* (Chicago: University of Chicago Press, 1968), 7.

The tales serve as a technique of social control by making acceptable and unacceptable behavior explicit.... The tales make it clear that law-breakers are punished and that their transgressions lie at the root of their misfortunes.

The tales ostensibly serve as guides of conduct. The Hasidim consciously use stories as the pleasantest way of introducing religious practices to the young.

From this we can draw some parallels between the Pueblo Indians and the Hasidim, along with many other peoples, in that these cultures hold their stories and the oral tradition in high regard as a valuable method of education.

Many of the Hasidic stories, such as "The Lost Princess"[18] and "The Seven Beggars,"[19] were told (and then printed at a much later time) as relatively simple tales, each with a plot that is easy to follow and which has intriguing suspense. However, the stories usually contain several levels of meaning. In his book, *Classic Hassidic Tales,*[20] Meyer Levin includes the following description in a triangular shape:

These tales contain wonders and mysteries that are hidden in
secret meanings, for not one word here written is without
deep purpose yet even the simple reader unlearned
in the secret of words may read these tales with
awakening, for their power is so great that no
man may read them in vain, and even the
simple man may see beyond their first
meaning and glimpse the eternal
delights and wonders in
the lightnings of their
truth.

The more one listens to and retells a Hasidic story, the more understanding and information one receives. Kabbalah, which originally denoted the oral tradition and which became transformed into the mystical tradition in the twelfth century, had a great influence and appeal in the Hasidic movement. Kabbalistic teachings note four levels of understanding. The first level is called *peshat*, which reveals the plot and the simple meaning of the story. The second level is called *remez*, which leads one to a lesson or the moral of the story. In other words, it is what one

---

18. Levin, *Classic Hassidic Tales,* 190-197.
19. *Ibid.,* 333-357.
20. *Ibid.,* 189.

takes away or deduces upon hearing the tale. The next higher level, the third, is called *derash*. Here the listener makes the connection with himself and sees the way in which the story relates to his own life. This level adds an exciting dimension to the text.

The fourth and highest level is called *sod*, which means secret. This level of understanding happens in a mysterious experiential way. Suddenly the meaning, the message, and the connectedness all become focused and integrated. The listener and the story become one.

Because folktales everywhere are shared, repeated, and passed on, they help to develop group identity and teach the values of that society. Storytelling becomes literally mind-expanding due to the mental images created by the language, and the cycle continues. The spoken word is a powerful, even magical, tool of the folk experience. Once again we see that the value of a tale lies in the telling.

Psychological Growth

The third feature of storytelling is that it offers the child the opportunity for psychological growth. Bruno Bettelheim articulates this idea in his book *The Uses of Enchantment: The Meaning and Importance of Fairy Tales*. He states that:[21]

> Today, as in times past, the most important and also the most difficult task in raising a child is helping him find meaning in life.... Regarding this task, nothing is more important than the impact of parents and others who take care of the child; second in importance is our cultural heritage, when transmitted to the child in the right manner. When children are young, it is literature that carries such information best.... In all these and many other respects, of the entire "children's literature" — with rare exceptions — nothing can be as enriching and as satisfying to child and adult alike as the folk fairy tale.

In other words, stories give the child a perspective and the ability to ask the "heart" questions: Who am I? What should I want? How should I act? Which are the values that I should internalize? This becomes a learning experience in the home, in the synagogue, and in the school.

A child needs to belong and to grow intellectually and emotionally. By hearing stories, a child, and indeed people of all ages, see and understand better their life pattern as a Jew and as a human being by sharing what has gone before and what is yet to come. A person is, after all, a sum total of his or her past and that past has to merge with the present and future to make life meaningful. When stories are reinterpreted and

---

21. Bruno Bettelheim, *The Uses of Enchantment* (New York: Alfred A. Knopf, 1976), 3-5.

relate to the listener's life, they have an impact on the mind. The language in the stories is a powerful tool which transmits both the meaning and the event.

However, we have to keep in focus that it is the art of the storyteller which makes the stories and the language come alive so that the past is projected into the present and achieves a viable and vital meaning for us. In turn, these stories promote cultural identity and self-knowledge. This can lead to the development of a conscious commitment to Judaism.

Here there is a definite connection between storytelling and theatre. Both use language. Both reach the imagination and feelings of a person who then responds intuitively to the experience. Although this response may be intellectual later on when applied to discussion and action, the emotions must be tapped at the outset. Storytelling, like theatre, entertains and also educates. What Charlotte Chorpenning says concerning the place of theatre in a child's life is also valid for and applicable to storytelling:[22]

> At a given moment in any play each child in any audience is a record of all his yesterdays, conscious or unconscious. Thus there is created within him a relatively stable pattern for interacting with the world around him.... Fortunately our patterns include an inborn urge for growth through experience. Good theatre is a near thing to life itself to feed this urge; it bombards patterns with vicarious interpreted experience. In life the final outcome of a definite experience may take an hour, a day, years or ages; a play can give the child an immediate experience in the final outcome of something he just saw happen. It thus helps to feed the inborn urge for growth through experience. When a child from four to forty watches a play, the whole orchestra of Self is playing—senses, nerves, glands, muscles, memories, intelligence, intellect, spirit. The experience builds into him dreams, desires, urges, new memories, perceptions—conscious and unconscious—that may flower in the next hour or in the far future. The whole experience is one of the organism-as-a-whole.

As we can see, stories give aesthetic pleasure and entertain us. In addition, stories teach and transmit a culture. On the one hand, stories tell us of past attitudes, ideas, and ideals, serving as a record of popular thought and life. On the other hand, stories serve as a reference point in a particular culture and can set norms for behavior and expectation. There is much wisdom in stories and a great use of sense experiences. The sharing of stories promotes group identity and values in a creative and inspiring way.

---

22. Charlotte Chorpenning, *Twenty-one Years with Children's Theatre* (Anchorage: Children's Theatre Press, 1955), 25-26.

Artistic creativity "is a plant that must be carefully and tenderly nurtured," says Mordecai Kaplan.[23] Storytelling, like a plant, produces seeds which are nurtured through the appeal to the senses, the folk experience, and the psychological needs of the child. It is the telling of Jewish tales and legends that offers the creative possibilities that serve as a bridge to educate and develop Jewish values and Jewish identity in our children.

What, then, do we find in these legends and tales of the Jewish people that, when told and retold, creates this bond and promotes "a sense of moral responsibility in action"? The values in Judaism are folk values in that they reflect collective rather than individual judgments. Kaplan discusses the folk sanctions and says,[24] "the *inner* aspect of the mores, laws and folkways which give character to a people consists of specific folk sanctions." These sancta give to a folk the state of self-awareness or self-consciousness. Kaplan continues: "They provide the folk with memory of its past and aspirations for the future, and so create the human differentia of group continuity and group history."

Telling stories gives the child a storehouse of memories from which to draw upon the values of his people. Because the values are presented in a form that is entertaining, aesthetic, and educational, the child attaches special importance to those values. The values in the stories give the child the aspirations for the future as an individual and as a member of a particular group who treasures these values.

Moral Value

The folklore of the Jews is distinguished from that of any other people by its monotheistic and ethical background. There is hardly a custom, a legend, a story, or a folksong that does not reflect the Jewish conviction of the existence of one God or that does not teach a moral lesson. In other words, Jewish folklore mirrors Jewish ethical conceptions. Some of the values in Judaism that have been passed down from generation to generation and which evolve in Judaism continually are: learning Torah, Jewish peoplehood, Shabbat, Israel, family, freedom, and *tzedakah*.

Let us now consider one of these values—learning Torah—as it is found in a story. By showing how important Torah is to the survival of the Jewish people in the form of a parable, the idea becomes inspiring and memorable. In addition, the story presents an example or role model to emulate in the person of Rabbi Akiba.

---

23. Kaplan, *Judaism as a Civilization*, 486.
24. *Ibid.*, 198.

It was the time of the Roman conquests. Jews were forbidden to study Torah and to remain Jews. However, Rabbi Akiba would not give up the study of Torah even when it meant certain death by the Roman soldiers. When asked why he would not stop, even to save his life, Rabbi Akiba answered with the following parable.

"A hungry fox was walking along the edge of a stream. Suddenly he noticed a silver fish swimming around in the stream.

" 'Little fish, beautiful silver fish, why do you swim around so fast?' the fox asked.

" 'Oh, I am trying to escape the fishermen's nets,' the fish replied.

" 'Well, then,' said the scheming fox, 'In that case, climb out of the water and get on my back. I'll carry you to safety!'

"The fox leaned over, ready to grab at the fish. But the fish swam quickly out of his reach and said:

" 'You are a sly one! What silly advice you are giving me! If I am in constant fear of my life in the water where I can live, how do you think I can survive on dry land where I cannot live at all? At least here in the water, I can try to avoid landing in the fishermen's nets and also getting caught by you.' And the fish swam away."

When Rabbi Akiba finished the story, he added:

"The Torah is a Jew's home, just as the water is a home for the fish. If we are in danger even when we study Torah, then our danger will be even greater if we stop studying Torah. We will be like fish out of water."

First of all, in this story-within-a-story, we have a fish who outwits the villain, the sly fox. Animals who talk and are clever have a special appeal to children. Children respond in a visceral way, especially to anything or anyone that is small and seemingly helpless like themselves. The Jew, accustomed to the role of the underdog, roots for the one less likely to win. Like the Jew, the fish wins through his use of reasoning. As the story is told, the listener pictures the scene and thus retains it in his mental picture gallery. Using the metaphor of water, a popular symbol in Jewish literature, the listener sees by extension how each one of us has to live according to who he is and where he belongs—like the fish who must live in water or the Jew who must live with Torah.

Let us consider another value—confession and atonement on Yom Kippur. As Kaplan writes,

> Yom Kippur is the day on which man should focus his attention upon the part that he plays as an individual in that world of which he is the center. The idea of repentance and consequent atonement...has been incorporated in the modern conception of moral responsibility.[25]

---

25. *Ibid.*, 449-450.

To this value we respond with affective regard after hearing this story:

> An angel, whom God punished for wrongdoing, was ordered to go
> to earth and to bring back the most precious thing he could find there.
> The angel first returned with a drop of blood from a soldier dying
> for his country. This was precious, but not the most precious.
>
> The angel flew back to earth and this time he came back with the last
> breath of a heroic woman who had sacrificed her life for others. This gift
> was also very precious, but still not the most precious.
>
> In despair, the angel flew everywhere looking and searching, when sud-
> denly he saw a criminal about to attack and kill an innocent man. At the
> very last moment, the criminal felt sorry for his victim. He repented and
> did not commit the terrible crime. Just at that moment, the attacker blinked,
> and a tear rolled down his cheek. The angel scooped up the tear and brought
> it back to Heaven. The "tear of repentance" was the most precious thing
> on earth, and the angel was forgiven. The angel was accepted once more
> in Heaven.

This story always brings tears to my eyes because it affects my emotions. The story builds in suspense with each precious offering. However,
it is the unexpected—the thing closest to the emotions—that is judged
the most precious and wins forgiveness for the angel. Again the child
identifies with the angel who has been punished. What child has not been
punished and has not sought forgiveness from the parent? And what
parent can harden his/her heart by not accepting the "tear of repentance"?
A child intuitively understands and remembers because the meaning
comes through vividly. Then the value presented in the story remains
forever as a gift of his heritage.

When I think about God, who is in each one of us, and about how
often our search for God takes us elsewhere instead of looking inside our
hearts, I think of the following two stories. In each of these stories, the
idea is made meaningful through an unusual situation which captures
the imagination. Here again, the value is learned and retained through
the art of the story.

The first story is told by Elie Wiesel in *Souls on Fire*.[26] It is attributed
to the Hasid Simha-Bunam of Pshishke, and also to Nahman of Bratzlav.

> The story tells of a poor Jew, Eizik son of Yekel, who lived in Cracow.
> One night he has a dream. In the dream he sees the capital city of
> Prague, and the voice in the dream tells him to go there for he would
> find a treasure under the bridge—a treasure that would solve all of
> his problems of poverty.

---

26. Wiesel, *Souls on Fire*, 203-205.

The dream appears three times and the voice keeps urging Eizik each time to go to Prague and dig for the treasure. After the third time, Eizik does go and finds the scene exactly as it had been in his dreams. But the palace guard approaches him before he could begin to dig and demands to know why he is there. Eizik, scared he will be arrested, blurts out the story of his dream of finding riches.

And so, he thought he was dreaming again when the dangerous captain burst out laughing.... "You Jews are even more stupid than I thought!... If I were as stupid as you, if I listened to voices, do you know where I would be at this very minute? In Cracow!... Imagine that for weeks and weeks, there was that voice at night telling me: 'There is a treasure waiting for you at the house of a Cracow Jew named Eizik, son of Yekel! Yes, under the stove!' Naturally, half the Jews there are called Eizik and the other half Yekel! And they all have stoves! Can you see me going from house to house, tearing down all the stoves, searching for a nonexistent treasure?"

Of course Eizik was not punished. Of course he hurried back home, moved the stove, and of course, he found the promised treasure. He paid his debts, married off his daughters, and as a token of his gratitude, built a synagogue that bears his name: Eizik, son of Yekel, a poor and pious Jew who remained pious even when he was no longer poor.

The second story is "The Princess Who Wanted to See God" from *Who Knows Ten* by Molly Cone.[27]

This story is about a princess who never cried because she got everything she ever wanted. The princess now demands to see God. Her father calls the Chief of Law and Order to carry out the command. He shows the princess the Book Of Laws and Punishments of the kingdom which he claims are "as good as God." But the princess is not satisfied. Then the Chief of the Treasury is ordered to carry out her command. He shows the princess the vault filled with gold. But again the princess is not satisfied. Finally the king himself begins to search for God so he can show God to the princess. As he wanders away from the palace, since he was unable to find God there, the king meets an old man who responds to a question and then adds, "God willing, that is." The king asks the old man to show God to the princess, and the old man agrees to try.

First the old man asks the princess to visit someone. The princess reluctantly goes with the old man to a small shabby cottage. When

27. Molly Cone, *Who Knows Ten* (New York: Union of American Hebrew Congregations, 1965), 14-20.

she steps inside, she meets a young girl who is very poor but smiling. When she discovers that this girl is crippled and cannot walk, the princess quickly leaves the cottage and follows the old man back to the palace.

When they reached the palace hall, the old man turned to her.

"Are you ready?" he asked.

"Ready? For what?" asked the princess. She had been so busy thinking of the other girl that she had forgotten all about herself.

The old man smiled. "...Now close your eyes, hold up this mirror, and look deep into your heart."

The princess closed her eyes and held up the mirror. Suddenly tears began to roll down the cheeks of the princess who had never cried. Big, soft, wet tears.

"Why are you crying?" asked the old man.

"I have been selfish all my life," she cried, "and I did not know it until I saw that poor girl." She put the mirror down and opened her eyes.

"Oh, sir, do you think it would help if I brought her some good soup, and maybe a pretty dress to wear? Do you think that would help?"

The old man smiled. He took the mirror from her hand and put it carefully away.

"You have seen God," he said.

After I tell this story, I lower my eyes and keep silent for a few moments. I know how this story affects me no matter how many times I have told it. I need time to make the transition to where I am physically. I know the listeners need the time, too. They have been on a journey with me. The have followed the search for God along with the princess, a young, self-centered, selfish, demanding child, like any one of the children in the audience at some time in their lives. The children now need private space and time to let the story settle into their minds and form the images in their mental storehouses.

The solution to the search is simply but effectively presented by the old man. He is an example, much needed in our society, of the older generation who has been there, and who has so much to teach us and to hand down to us about the way we need to conduct our lives.

In this story, as in the story dealing with atonement, the tear is the important symbol of understanding and repentance. Through the symbol of the tear, a child can visualize the situation, identify with the character, understand the meaning of the story, and learn the kernel of the story— its meaning or value. All of this is accomplished not in a lecture format, but in a creative, imaginative, but also traditional way: through a story. A story gives hope. A story shows the possibilities. A story is life-fulfilling. A child listening to this story is able to react with *empathy*; that is, with understanding, identification, appreciation, and a capacity to respond.

Returning to the story at the beginning of this essay, we see it has a king and a princess, as in the last story. A king and a princess are often found as characters in Jewish stories. The king can represent God in an earthly form. The daughter can be the Shekhinah, the Presence of God. The wine can stand for our own resources. Symbols can be interpreted in many ways and on many levels. What is wonderful is that each one of us brings to the story his ideas and feelings and, if truly open to the experience, takes away a richer treasure of ideas and feelings. The story, enhanced by the voice of a storyteller, becomes a shared experience and reaches the listener in the inner recesses of the mind and heart. When the listener puts the whole mind and imagination into the listening experience, he takes out even more. In this way, each person does make a difference.

A recurrent theme in *Judaism as a Civilization* is that the worth of a civilization depends not only upon the ideals and values it professes, but upon its ability to energize them. First, the Jewish children must know the ideals and values in order to internalize them. Then they can act on them in situations, which should always be presented. The aim of stories is to give an opportunity to children to develop a touchstone for their imaginative strength, communicative powers, and sense of order and beauty in the world. The aim of storytelling is to create a trust and bond between the teller and the listener so that true education happens.

Storytelling is uniquely suited for the type of education we now require because it transmits Jewish culture. It creates a medium in which we can help children grapple with the meaning of values in a Jewish setting. This in turn may profoundly affect their sense of Jewish identity.

Sources for Jewish Stories

Adler, David A. *Children's Treasury of Chassidic Tales*. New York: Mesorah, 1983.

Ausubel, Nathan, ed. *A Treasury of Jewish Folklore*. New York: Crown Publishers, 1948.

————————. *A Treasury of Jewish Humor*. New York: Doubleday & Co., 1951.

Barash, Asher. *A Golden Treasury of Jewish Tales*. New York: Dodd, Mead, & Co., 1966.

Belth, Norton, ed. *The World Over Story Book*. New York: Bloch Publishing Co., 1952.

Bin Gorion, Micha Josef. *Mimekor Yisrael: Classical Jewish Folktales*. Indiana: Indiana University Press, 1976.

Brodie, Deborah, ed. *Stories My Grandfather Should Have Told Me*. New York: Bonim Books, 1977.

Cone, Molly. *Who Knows Ten*. New York: Union of American Hebrew Congregations, 1965.

Einhorn, David. *The Seventh Candle and Other Folk Tales of Eastern Europe*. New York: KTAV Publishing House, Inc., 1968.

Eisenberg, Azriel, ed. *Bar Mitzvah Treasury*. New York: Behrman House, 1969.

Eisenberg, Azriel and Leah Ain Globe. *The Secret Weapon and Other Stories of Faith and Valor*. New York: The Soncino Press, 1966.

Freehof, Lillian S. *Stories of King David*. Philadelphia: The Jewish Publication Society of America, 1952.

Freehof, Lillian S. *Stories of King Solomon*. Philadelphia: The Jewish Publication Society of America, 1955.

Gold, Sharlya. *The Potter's Four Sons*. New York: Doubleday & Co., 1970.*

Goodman, Philip, ed. *The Hanukkah Anthology*. Philadelphia: The Jewish Publication Society of America, 1976.

_____, ed. *The Passover Anthology*. Philadelphia: The Jewish Publication Society of America, 1961.

_____, ed. *The Purim Anthology*. Philadelphia: The Jewish Publication Society of America, 1973.

_____, ed. *The Sukkot and Simhat Torah Anthology*. Philadelphia: The Jewish Publication Society of America, 1973.

Harlow, Jules, ed. *Lessons from Our Living Past*. New York: Behrman House, 1972.

Howe, Irving and Eliezer Greenberg. *A Treasury of Yiddish Stories*. New York: The Viking Press, 1954.

_____, ed. *Selected Stories of I. L. Peretz*. New York: Schocken Books, 1974.

Ish-Kishor, Judith. *Tales from the Wise Men of Israel*. New York: J. B. Lippincott Company, 1962.

Klapholtz, Yisroel Yaakov. *Tales of the Baal Shem Tov*. New York: Feldheim Publishers, 1970.

Kranzler, Gershon. *The Golden Shoes and Other Stories*. New York: Philipp Feldheim, Inc., 1960.

Levin, Meyer. *Classic Hassidic Tales*. New York: Penguin Paperback Books, 1975.

Levitin, Sonia. *A Sound to Remember*. New York: Harcourt Brace Jovanovich, 1979.*

Millgram, Abraham E., ed. *Sabbath*. Philadelphia: The Jewish Publication Society of America, 1944.

Nahmad, N. M. *A Portion in Paradise and Other Folktales*. New York: W. W. Norton & Co., 1970.

Noy, Dov, ed. *Folktales of Israel*. Chicago: The University of Chicago Press, 1963.

Posy, Arnold. *Israeli Tales and Legends*. New York: Jonathan David Publisher, 1966.

Prose, Francine. *Stories from our Living Past*. New York: Behrman House, 1974.

Rush, Barbara and Eliezer Marcus. *Seventy and One Tales for the Jewish Year: Folk Tales for the Festivals*. New York: American Zionist Youth Foundation, 1980.

Schloss, Ezekiel and Morris Epstein, eds. *The New World Over Storybook*. New York: Bloch Publishing Co., 1968.

Schram, Peninnah. *A Storyteller's Journey* (record album/cassette). New York: POM Records, 1977.

Schram, Peninnah. *Elijah's Violin and Other Jewish Fairy Tales* (record album/cassette). New York: POM Records, 1977.

Schwartz. Howard. *Elijah's Violin and Other Jewish Fairy Tales*. New York: Harper and Row, 1983.

Serwer, Blanche Luria. *Let's Steal the Moon*. Boston: Little Brown & Co., 1970.

Simms, Laura and Ruth Kozodoy. *Exploring Our Living Past*. New York: Behrman House, Inc., 1979.

Simon, Solomon. *The Wise Men of Helm and Their Merry Tales*. New York: Behrman House, 1945.

_____. *More Wise Men of Helm*. New York: Behrman House, 1965.

_____. *The Wandering Beggar*. New York: Behrman House, 1942.

Singer, Isaac Bashevis. *Mazel and Schlimazel or the Milk of a Lioness*. New York: Farrar, Straus & Giroux, Inc., 1967.*

_____. *Zlateh the Goat*. New York: Harper & Row, 1966.

_____. *When Shlemiel Went to Warsaw*. New York: Farrar, Straus & Giroux, 1968.

_____. *The Power of Light*. New York: Farrar, Straus & Giroux, 1980.

_____. *Stories for Children*. New York: Farrar, Straus & Giroux, 1984.

Sobel, Samuel, ed. *A Treasury of Sea Stories*. New York: Jonathan David, 1965.

Soyer, Abraham. *The Adventures of Yemina and Other Stories*. New York: The Viking Press, 1979.

Tenenbaum, Samuel. *The Wise Men of Chelm*. New York: Collier Books, 1975.

---

* Indicates a book that contains one story only. All the other books listed contain many stories.

Doing Justice to Tzedakah:
Towards a Complete
Theory and Practice

■ ■ ■ Jeffrey L. Schein

Imagine for a moment a synagogue school which has succeeded in instilling generous habits of giving *tzedakah* in its students. At a nearby temple, teachers and principals labor to create a model *tzedakah* lesson which conveys to students the ethical dynamics implicit in the *tzedakah* ladder of the Rambam. Down the block a bit at a modern shul, a rabbi insists that real *tzedakah* must be wedded to the element of human contact one finds in the Jewish notion of *gemilut hasadim*. Appropriate community projects are designed which help students transform the anonymous giving of *tzedakah* into intimate deeds of lovingkindness.

The three approaches to the teaching of *tzedakah* in the ideal Jewish neighborhood described above are, in fact, representative of three creative approaches to the topic found among Jewish educators today. It is the thesis of this paper that, though each approach is legitimate, each alone is a fragmentary representation of the meaning of *tzedakah*. In fact, the traditional Jewish teaching about *tzedakah* is richer and more complete than any of the three approaches.

What follows is an attempt to sketch some of the conceptual, developmental, and programmatic components of an effective approach towards the teaching of *tzedakah*. In each area, materials are provided at the end of the article. The materials have proved effective in various educational settings. The emphasis of this paper is on explicating the various Jewish and educational dimensions of *tzedakah*. The concern with breadth of vision means that each dimension described needs a great deal more elaboration. Nevertheless, if the paper helps Jewish educators see the whole picture of what is involved in teaching about *tzedakah*, its basic purpose will be served. A greater degree of justice will be done to the teaching of *tzedakah*.

The Conceptual Domain of Tzedakah

What is *tzedakah*? What distinguishes it, on the one hand, from an ethical concern which Jews and non-Jews might share and, on the other, from other important Jewish concepts like *hasidut* and *rahamim*? It is only with answers to such questions that teachers can bring clarity to the task of teaching students about *tzedakah*.

Most of us can agree upon a negative definition of *tzedakah*. We can say what it is not. *Tzedakah* is not charity in the Christian sense of a praiseworthy act of self-sacrifice (in imitation of Jesus). Nor is it "charity" in the American philanthropical mold of caring for the less fortunate. The derivation of *tzedakah* from the Hebrew root *tzedek* (meaning justice) shines too clearly through both the philosophical and folk usages of *tzedakah* to allow for such confusion.

Thus, most conceptual understandings of *tzedakah* begin with the notion that *tzedakah* is an untranslatable blend of charity and righteousness. This explanation of the meaning of *tzedakah* is correct as far as it goes, but the conceptual geography of the term *tzedakah* includes a broader domain. My own formula (assuredly not complete or authoritative) includes the following elements:

TZEDAKAH = CHARITY + JUSTICE + RELIGIOUS RESPONSIBILITY + JEWISH HUMOR + RESPONSIBILITY TO THE TOTALITY OF JEWISH CIVILIZATION

The following Hasidic tale (Newman, *Hasidic Anthology*, p. 33) evokes the elements of religious responsibility and Jewish humor in the *tzedakah* formula.

> A woman and a man came to Rabbi Phineas Hurwitz of Frankfort with complaints. The woman's lament was that her husband was over-generous in his charities, and the man's complaint was that his rich brother refused to give him any assistance whatsoever. Both defendants were summoned into the presence of the Rabbi.
>
> The husband offered as his defense the fact that he feared an early death, and wished to acquire a great store of good deeds for the profit of his soul.

The brother defended himself by saying that he feared to give away any portion of his wealth lest he have insufficient for his old age.

The Rabbi rendered his decision as follows: "May the Lord protect you both from that which you fear."

This decision was deemed just by the Lord. The philanthropist who feared a short life, lived until a ripe old age, and the miser who was afraid of living too long, was soon summoned by death.

Tzedakah implies a religious responsibility for the way we live our lives. Something more than a utilitarian calculus of helping others and society is involved. Our character is ultimately at stake in the way we practice or do not practice *tzedakah*. Ironically, this serious spiritual concern — metaphorically depicted in the Hasidic tale as a matter of life and death — is tempered with an element of Jewish folk humor. The subtle humor and irony in the tale is amplified in the shtetl traditions of the *shnorrer* bargaining for his inalienable right to *tzedakah*. Like everything else in Judiasm, *tzedakah* is approached with a blend of challenge for man to become all that he can be as a creature made *betzelem Elohim* (in the image of God) and a recognition of our human frailties.

The final element in the formula for *tzedakah* is responsibility for the totality of our Jewish religious civilization. The Jewish and non-Jewish poor are certainly important recipients of *tzedakah*. Yet Jewish philanthrophy is justifiably concerned with the spiritual and cultural survival of Judaism as well as the physical survival of all human beings. *Tzedakah* is ultimately the action correlated with anything we might study in our curriculum. An example of how *tzedakah* projects might be correlated with the many different aspects of Judaism as a religious civilization is included in Appendix A. It is from a program originally developed at the Ann Spak Thal School of Society Hill Synagogue in Philadelphia.

Developmental Aspects of Tzedakah

There are three fundamental educational dimensions involved in the moral development of our Jewish children: ethical analysis, Jewish interpretation, and personal interpretation. Ethical analysis is essentially the task of understanding the principles which guide the performance of a moral act. The work of Lawrence Kohlberg has emphasized this dimension of values education.[1] Jewish interpretation is the process by which a particular Jewish value becomes integrated into a wider complex of Jewish

---

1. See L. Kohlberg and C. Gilligan, "The Adolescent as a Philosopher: The Discovery of Self in a Post-Conventional World," *Daedalus: Journal of the American Academy of Arts and Sciences* 100 (1971):1051-1086.

values and concretizes itself in specific historical and behavioral situations. Max Kadushin addressed this process in a scholarly fashion.[2] Jewish *midrash* and *aggadah* illustrate how well the process functions in a traditional Jewish context. Personal interpretation focuses on the meaning and value which individuals attach to what has already been sanctioned by tradition. Much of the "affective" work in Jewish education has emphasized this dimension of Jewish values.

All three dimensions are essential for an effective approach to teaching *tzedakah*. It is important, in an analytic vein, for students to understand why giving in such a way as to make a *tzedakah* recipient independent (the highest step on Rambam's ladder) is the highest form of giving. Students need to be able to articulate the moral reasons underlying their feelings and intuitions. It is crucial from the point of view of Jewish interpretation for students to recognize the changing textures of Jewish civilization which have added nuances or new values to older Jewish concepts. An explanation of how *Keren Ami* became a form of *tzedakah* as Jews resettled Eretz Yisrael at the turn of the century is an important task of Jewish interpretation. In a more traditional exegetical sense, an explanation of the way that Jacob becomes transformed from a heel (in the biblical account) who steals Esau's blessings to the *tzaddik* who was preparing lentils for his father after the death of Abraham (in the later rabbinic account) is part of the interpretive teaching of *tzedakah*.

Neither of the above two dimensions touches on the crucial realm of how one feels about *tzedakah* in a personal way. Many Jewish adults today have strong positive or negative feelings about the *pushke* which was provided for them (or pushed at them) as a child. The feelings still exercise a powerful influence on their present practice (or lack of it) of *tzedakah*. A concern with whether our constant extolling of the value of *tzedakah* actually affects students in a positive way is another crucial part of the teaching of *tzedakah*.

In general, Jewish educators concerned with values education have emphasized one of these three aspects of *tzedakah*. Many Reform Jewish educators, in keeping with their "affective" orientation, have focused on the element of personal interpretation. Orthodox Jewish educators are still likely to emphasize the exegetical domain because of its connection with traditionally sanctioned modes of Jewish interpretation. Many Conservative Jewish educators, influenced by the analytic orientation of the Melton Center,[3] have favored the analytic dimension of teaching about *tzedakah*.

---

2. Max Kadushin, *The Rabbinic Mind* (New York: Bloch, 1972), 14-26.
3. Available from the Melton Research Center of The Jewish Theological Seminary of America (New York) is a curriculum on the teaching of *tzedakah* and *gemilut hasadim*.

In fact, no one dimension of teaching about *tzedakah* is more important than another. Included at the end of the article in Appendices B, C, and D are examples of teaching about *tzedakah* in each of the three essential modes. While the task of integrating these approaches into a coherent curriculum about *tzedakah* is beyond the scope of this article, the fundamental point remains the same: any such curriculum which does not address all three dimensions is not doing justice to the Jewish concept of *tzedakah*.

Programmatic Aspects of Tzedakah: The Domain of Ma'aseh (Action)

The last dimension of *tzedakah* teaching worthy of exploration is the domain of action. To the extent that Judaism measures the worth of our characters by our deeds rather than our words, it is perhaps the most essential aspect of *tzedakah*. It is a realm with possibilities as broad as the imagination and creativity of Jewish educators who wish to open up new possibilities for holiness through the giving of *tzedakah*.

Included at the end of this article (Appendices E and F) are two letters which reflect some of the efforts at Congregation Emanu El in San Bernardino to involve the family in *tzedakah*. The first is a letter to parents trying to alert them to the role they play in shaping their child's attitude towards *tzedakah*. More concretely, the letter suggests a "ladder of *tzedakah* giving" with appropriate levels for each family to join. Also included in this letter are suggestions for how teachers and principals might model *tzedakah* giving.

The second letter is to a group of parents who wanted to be involved in a special *tzedakah* project. Their children were given an opportunity to make their own *tzedakah* boxes. As holidays approached, parents and children were sent a letter with suggestions about where the money they had collected as a family might be sent.

The above project began with children of kindergarten age. In this regard, one final programmatic aspect of *tzedakah* is important. Much of what educators call "character" or "moral personality" is shaped before a child enters formal Jewish schooling. With our own child Benjamin (now six) we have tried to begin teaching about *tzedakah* early. Each year, in honor of Benjamin's birthday, we make two *tzedakah* donations – each in the dollar amount of his years – one to a Jewish cause and one to a non-Jewish cause. At age three we began to talk with him about where the money is going. Eventually, in ways appropriate to his age and developmental capacities, he will assume responsibility for writing the letters accompanying the money and for deciding where the money will go. In this way we hope Benjamin will write his own *pesukim*, on the model of

Pirkei Avot, about the role of the *tzedakah* in the Jewish life cycle (at age two we give..., at five..., etc.).

There are surely other ways to bring the world of *tzedakah* home to Jewish children. The important thing for both teacher and parent is that it indeed be a world which reflects the richness of what Judaism and studies of human personality have to say about the art of giving. Pale imitations or models based on effective yet fragmentary methodologies do not do justice to *tzedakah*.

Appendix A: TZEDAKAH AND JEWISH CIVILIZATION

Tzedakah is often treated solely as a matter of building the right habits of generosity and concern for one's fellow Jews. There is, however, another dimension of *tzedakah*. It is the dimension which involves decision making. At the Thal School, we have tried to develop this dimension by involving the students in making decisions about our *tzedakah* money. Together as a class we decide where to send our money.

The procedure we follow is sketched below. At the end of a unit of study, we have a meeting. One teacher has the responsibility of presenting three different options to the class about where to send the money. These are all related to the theme we have been studying in the school. We then discuss the various options. The discussions often lead to important explorations of what it really means to help someone.

Tzedakah as a concept and as a value is explored. The nice thing is that, because we are really deciding what to do with the *tzedakah* money, the discussion is quite free-flowing and comfortable. There is a reality orientation to it that would be missing if we chose to talk about *tzedakah* as a separate unit. Several examples of our *tzedakah* assemblies, along with the value issues that came up in the course of discussion, are:

1. Life in Biblical Times
   Options Presented:
   a. A donation to the Israel Museum.
   b. A donation to University of Pennsylvania Museum.
   c. A donation to an Israel "nature" group trying to preserve Bedouin culture.

   Issues which emerged in values discussion:
   a. Is it better to help Jews and Jewish groups here in America?
   b. Is it better to help institutions that preserve the past or living groups of people?
   c. Can we help Bedouins even though they are Arabs?

2. Soviet Jewry
   Options Presented:
   a. A donation to the local Soviet Jewry Council.
   b. A donation to a local Russian Jewish family.

    c. Using our money to purchase items ourselves which we would give to a congregant traveling to the Soviet Union, who could smuggle the items to refuseniks.

Issues which emerged in values discussion:
    a. Is it better to give to institutions that are "experts" in what's going on, or to try something ourselves?
    b. Is it better to give to a group that can decide who needs the help most, or to give it to people you know?
    c. Is it okay to help some people by doing something illegal (smuggling)?

It should be clear that the teacher's choice of options tends to structure the dilemmas that the discussion will explore.

Appendix B: THE ANALYTIC APPROACH TO TZEDAKAH

Rambam's Ladder (For Junior High Students)

Maimonides felt that not all kinds of *tzedakah* were of equal value. Below you will find Rambam's *tzedakah* ladder (running from the lowest to the highest form of *tzedakah*) and some suggested exercises for helping students probe the underlying moral principles which set up the *tzedakah* ladder as it is. Before doing them, however, students should be given an opportunity to order the various types of *tzedakah* behavior into their own ladder. The best way of doing this would be to break down into groups of three to five, giving each group eight pieces of posterboard, each with a different kind of *tzedakah* on it. These groups must arrange the pieces from lowest to highest on the basis of decisions they come to as a group. They can later compare this with Rambam's ladder, and be led in a discussion exploring the differences between their ladders and the ladder of Rambam.

    It is also valuable, subsequent to this exercise, to have each group work on a second type of *tzedakah* ladder, in which the rungs are particular acts of *tzedakah* in which the local Jewish community is typically engaged.

Rambam's Ladder

1. To give but sadly.
2. To give less than is fitting but in good humor.
3. To give only after having been asked to give.
4. To give before being asked.
5. To give in such a manner that the donor does not know who the recipient is.
6. To give in such a manner that the recipient does not know who the donor is.
7. To give in such a way that neither the donor nor the recipient knows the identity of the other.
8. To give not alms but to help poor become independent through taking them into partnership, employing them, or some other means.

Thoughts and Questions About Rambam's Ladder

If *tzedakah* were only a matter of giving money, Rambam's ladder wouldn't be concerned with _____ and _____.

Maimonides would probably say of someone who didn't care to think about which kinds of *tzedakah* are most admirable (of someone who said he would just give when he felt like it), _____.

Maimonides was very concerned that the amount of *tzedakah* be adequate for the recipient's needs. But he also said that one was forbidden to give too much *tzedakah*. From the ladder and your own hunches, why do you think Maimonides said this?

The reason that giving sadly is at the lowest rung of the ladder is _____.

The reason that giving in a way that makes someone independent is the highest rung is _____.

The sixth rung of the ladder is superior to the fifth because _____.

The fourth rung of the ladder is better than the third because _____.

The seventh rung is higher than the fifth or sixth because _____.

One Final Exercise

Suppose you met a beggar. Where on Rambam's ladder would you be ranked if you responded to the beggar in the following ways:

1. If you gave him no *tzedakah* at all?
2. If you gave him some money because you thought it would get rid of him?
3. If you followed him home, saw where he lived and later took a package of food goods over to his house and left it there?
4. If you invited him to come to dinner with you?
5. If you sent him a notice from your company of a job opportunity, and wrote in a way that it appeared it had not been written especially for him?
6. If you lectured him about being lazy?

A Project

Have students take a look at their own Jewish community. What kind of *tzedakah* does it engage in? Where does it fall on Rambam's ladder? How could it be elevated a rung or two?

Appendix C: THE PERSONAL INTERPRETATION OF TZEDAKAH

The Giving Tree

Purpose

The Giving Tree by Shel Silverstein, is a wonderful story about giving. It tells of a tree and the great satisfaction it derives from being able to give of itself (fruit, shade, etc.). It powerfully evokes the notion that *tzedakah* (compassion for others) is not self-sacrifice, but is rather self-fulfillment.

This lesson is divided into two parts. The first attempts to help students appreciate the story through guided questions. The second section is a suggested project that will help keep the image of a "Giving Tree" in front of the students as the year progresses.

Questions

After reading the story to children, the following questions might be explored:

How did you like the story? Did it give you anything?

What makes giving so special? Can you think of a time you felt really good about giving?

The tree kept getting smaller as he gave things to the boy. You would think the tree would begin to feel weak and little. But each time it gave it felt stronger and better. What is there about giving which makes us feel stronger even when we have less after doing it?

Did the boy appreciate the tree more or less as he grew older?

How do you think the tree felt when the boy (now an older man) said, "I'm too big to climb trees."

Was the boy a good giver?

Of all the things that the tree gave the boy (play, shade, leaves, wood for a house, and a stump to sit on) which was the best gift?

The tree also took. It took the sun, the rain, and minerals from nature. We're all both givers and takers in life. What were the boy and tree—bigger takers or bigger givers? What are you?

Unlike the Giving Tree, I'd never be able to _____.

Like the Giving Tree, I _____.

Two Projects

Make two "giving trees" for your students (or let the students make them). Let one be a Giving Tree, pure and simple. Make the leaves of the Giving Tree big enough so that as weeks go on students can put down (and then discuss) the kinds of acts of giving that they do in their own lives.

Make another tree the Jewish Giving Tree. On its leaves, let students write all the things which Judaism gives us as Jews.

Appendix D: THE JEWISH INTERPRETIVE AND ANALYTIC APPROACH TO TZEDAKAH

The Helmites Purchase a Barrel of Justice

Purpose

The Helmites always make what philosophers call "category mistakes." In the story, "How the Helmites Bought a Barrel of Justice,"[4] the Helmites engage in "the myth of misplaced concreteness." Frustrated that justice does not exist in their own community, they begin to search for justice in a tangible form, a barrel. They treat *tzedakah* — a concept, a process, and a human action — as if it were a thing. To catch the Helmites' mistake, students need to understand that justice is created and not pre-existent. Most children over eight will catch the Helmites' mistake and laugh heartily at it because they do have such a concept.

There are two parts to this lesson. The first is to tell the story and let it lead into a discussion of what *tzedakah* really is in the non-Helm world. The second part uses the notion of a barrel of justice, which really pokes fun at the Helmites, to our educational advantage. Using the barrel of justice as an ongoing visual representation, students can be asked to place into it the symbolic values and actions which make *tzedakah* part of the ever-changing life of the Jewish people.

The Story

The key to telling the story is to build up the fact that in a Helm story everything makes perfect sense once the initial mistake has been made. The students' job is to look out for that one wrong idea that turns the whole story on its head and makes the Helmites such lovable fools. The natural discussion question is, "Well, if *tzedakah* isn't a barrel of justice, what is it?" My experience is that the rest takes care of itself if the teacher simply encourages open discussion in response to the question. Good storytelling technique (pantomime, telling rather than reading the story, etc.) builds up the ridiculousness of the Helmites and sets the stage for a good discussion.

The "Barrel" Follow-Up

The fondness which kids have for this story can become the basis for a continuing discussion about *tzedakah*. Some area on the wall should be cleared where a number of large posterboard barrels can be displayed. Above all the barrels can be the words "*Tzedakah*: Not a Barrel of Magic or a Barrel of Fish But..." The barrels underneath can vary, but I would suggest the following:

---

4. Solomon Simon, "How the Helmites Bought a Barrel of Justice," *The Wise Men of Helm* (Behrman House, 1973), 67-76.

A Symbol Barrel: Drawn or pasted onto it are the representations of the symbol that captures the real meaning of *tzedakah*. A picture of the human heart, a dollar bill, and the Torah are some of the things that students might come up with. Symbols can be added as the year goes on.

A "Justice Now" and "Justice Then" Set of Barrels: Students can be given responsibility to bring in newspaper clippings which exemplify "Justice Now." The teacher should take the lead in bringing in examples of justice as it was practiced in the past.

Several other sets of barrels can be used to involve students in the analytical domain of *tzedakah*. The "conceptual geography" of what *tzedakah* is and what it is not can be explored with displays of:

A Monkey Barrel, with examples of actions which are definitely not acts of *tzedakah* or justice.

A Tzedakah and a Gemilut Hasadim Barrel, focussed on the difference between the two.

Appendix E: LETTER TO PARENTS

Dear Parents:

During the second half of the year, I would like to ask for your cooperation with two special projects. The first is *tzedakah*. *Tzedakah* is a difficult word to translate (it's a blend of justice and charity that can't really be captured in English), and an even more difficult concept to teach about. We are trying to do our part in the school. We have discussed at our faculty meetings ways of making *tzedakah* more than just the mechanical giving of nickels and dimes. Some classes are bringing in clothes, toys, and canned goods rather than just money. All classes will be involved in special sessions with me about the real meaning of *tzedakah* (emphasizing the importance of the intention as well as the act), and near the end of the year all students will be taken through a decision-making process of choosing which organization to give our *tzedakah* money to.

You can help us make *tzedakah* a meaningful part of your child's Jewish education. Below is "Rabbi Schein's Family *Tzedakah* Ladder." It's not as elegant as Maimonides' classical eight rungs. Nor is it as important, since it only deals with the financial and not the interpersonal aspects of *tzedakah*. But it is something only you, the parents, can control. Teachers and principals can't realistically take responsibility for this aspect of *tzedakah* without unfairly embarrassing children for things over which the children have no control.

The First Rung

Sit down with your children and talk with them about their allowance. If they are willing, set up the following "Matching Fund" arrangement. If they are willing to put so much (nickel, dime, or quarter—the amount isn't important) money toward *tzedakah* each week, you as parent(s) will contribute an equal amount. They can bring the money each Sunday to the School for Jewish Living or to Mid-Week Hebrew classes.

The Second Rung

Have your child "earn" some extra money for *tzedakah* by doing some task around the house on a weekly basis that is not part of his or her present responsibilities.

The Third Rung

Commit yourself as a family to collecting *tzedakah* money before you sit down to your Friday night dinner. If you have a traditional Shabbat, this will add a new dimension to it. We will make time within the school for your child to make a special *tzedakah* box. On a monthly basis, Rabbi Cohn and I will send you some suggestions of what might be a particularly good *tzedakah* project for that period of time. There will be more than one choice, so you can decide as a family where the money will be sent.

At the end of this letter is a special form for you to send back to us if you are interested and willing to do *tzedakah* at the dizzying spiritual heights of the third rung. I want to emphasize that though the ladder is a hierarchy for fairly good and obvious reasons, the important thing is that you let your child know that you know about *tzedakah* and that you are concerned. Please jump on our ladder at any point where you're comfortable.

Aside from my ladder, there are three other ways that you can help with *tzedakah*. One is just to communicate with your children. Tell them when you've given money to a worthy organization. Tell them why you thought it was a worthwhile group. It's even appropriate, when you are confronted with your yearly dilemma of how much to give for your United Jewish Welfare Fund pledge, to talk about it with your children.

The second is that, beginning with the second semester of the school year, we will have three cartons out in the hallway: one for old toys, one for old clothes, and one for canned goods. Please send things to the temple which you and your children have around the house but are not using. Again, it is important for you as well as us to let your children know that you think this is a worthwhile endeavor.

Finally, in regard to *tzedakah*, I invite you to share in my neurosis. Some of your children, particularly those in the Mid-Week Hebrew classes, may have intimated that Rabbi Schein is a chronic gambler. I'm afraid it's true. I will offer to put this wager to students: If they can perform some small talk in Hebrew, I will donate so much money (usually a penny or two, but I've been known to go as high as a dime in these inflationary times). It's a lot of fun and does remind the students about *tzedakah*. There is an even more important educational point behind it, however. I want to convey to them that the act of giving to *tzedakah* has none of the pious and Puritan overtones to it that American philanthropical modes addict us to. *Tzedakah* is not given just to "help the less fortunate." It's considered a positive mitzvah. The Talmud indicates that we'd be obligated to give *tzedakah* even if there were no poor, for the elevating effect it has on our characters.

I invite you to sublimate your latent gambling fetishes in the same way I have. Enclosed in this letter is a puzzle with the names of eighty-nine prominent Jews, past and present, hidden within it. See if you and those children in your family who are old enough to help can find as many of those personalities as possible. Put their names down on a separate sheet. Send the puzzle, the sheet, and a nickel for each personality you find to school with your child. You can send a check to Congregation Emanu El if, God willing, you do well. Just to add a little spice to your effort, I'll donate a dollar to *tzedakah* for any family that can find seventy-five or more of the persons.

Sincerely,
Rabbi Jeffrey Schein

Appendix F

Letter sent to families who participated in the Third Rung of the *Tzedakah* program (see Appendix E).

Dear _____,

First, I want to thank you for participating on the "highest rung" of the *tzedakah* ladder. I hope Scott, Ari, Liana, and Charlie all enjoyed making their *tzedakah* boxes. I also hope that they are adding something to your family celebration of Shabbat or whatever other time you have been using them. As I indicated in my original letter, I'm now getting in touch to pose a question for you as individual families: namely, what to do with the *tzedakah* money you have collected. Let me make three suggestions to you. I hope you'll talk it out as a family. I would be very interested to hear what you decide and how the discussion goes. My three suggestions follow:

Kosher Meals for the Elderly

This group travels around and provides kosher meals for Jews in Los Angeles who cannot get them otherwise. At Pesah time they provide kosher for Passover meals and also plenty of matzah. This group does receive special funding from the Los Angeles federation but presumably could use the extra money to make a special Passover gift of food to an elderly person (address included).

Habad House, Shemura Matza

Habad is the group that made special presents of baskets of food to the Sunday school for Purim. They make *shemura* matzah for Passover and distribute it to those who need it. *Shemura* matzah is different from regular kosher matzah in that the wheat is watched from the time it is harvested until the time the matzah is made to make sure that it does not come into contact with any leavened substance. It is also made by hand (address included).

American Association for Ethiopian Jews

At Passover, we should become especially aware of our responsibility to help Jews who still live in "bondage." The black Jews of Ethiopia, perhaps the oldest surviving group of Jews (also known as Falashas), are facing ecological and political disaster. The new regime in Ethiopia has dealt harshly with them, and they are barely able to eke out a living as farmers. The association is trying to help them through direct aid and by helping American Jews to understand the plight of the Falashas (address included).

Shalom and Best
Wishes for a Good Pesah,
Rabbi Jeffrey Schein

Additional Resources Recommended for Teaching About Tzedakah

Ross, Lillian. *Tzedakah: Not Charity But Justice*. Miami: Central Agency for Jewish Education, 1977.
Siegel, Danny. *Gym Shoes and Irises*. Spring Valley, NY: Town House Press, 1982.

Faith in God After the Holocaust:
An Educational Encounter

■ ■ ■ Jeffrey L. Schein

The theological problems created for Jewish hearts and minds by the Holocaust are enormous. It is indeed difficult to "love the Lord your God with all your heart, all your soul, and all your might" if one entertains even the slightest suspicion that God sat silently by as six million Jews died. Numerous Jewish thinkers have addressed the central question. The responses range from those who feel that faith in God must be retained (Fackenheim, for instance) to those who feel that the traditional conception of the relationship between man and God must be fundamentally altered because of the Holocaust (for instance, Rubenstein).

What follows in this paper is a description of a program designed to help Jews grapple with the theological problems posed by the Holocaust. The program was originally designed for a teen *kallah*. It has subsequently been used in such diverse settings as a camp staff program for Tisha B'Av, a discussion group for Jewish inmates at a prison, and various adult education programs. Each setting demands new adaptations, but the key elements of the program remain constant: that is, the dramatic encounter and the conceptual clarity and simplicity about the theological positions of each of the thinkers.

The Educational Program: An Appropriate Encounter
for Jewish Adolescents

My own thinking about an appropriate program about the Holocaust for Jewish adolescents began in the negative. I was most aware of what I objected to in the way theology and the Holocaust are commonly presented to Jewish teenagers. In looking back on the program, the following criticisms of contemporary Holocaust and theological teaching guided my preparation:

1. The Holocaust is often used (or misused) as a leverage point in moving the Jewish adolescent towards a firmer Jewish identity. The sheer power and drama of the event can shake Jewish teenagers out of their general complacency about their Jewishness. The emotional impact of the Holocaust thus becomes the major focus of the teaching.

But all effective teaching is confluent: That is, it emphasizes both feeling and thinking, and seeks to explore the interrelationship between the two. Only recently have Holocaust curricula begun to do this.

2. Young Jewish adolescents can think about abstract issues of theology. But they cannot think about the issues abstractly. The intellectual gift of conceptual (or, in Piaget's terms, "operational") thinking is fairly precarious for a fourteen-year-old. The theological issues which would emerge in the program need to be presented in a concrete and immediate way.

3. In considering the theological issues, more than the intellectual and emotional development of the student as an individual learner was involved. The sociological context in which their Jewish identity unfolded was also crucial.

Jewish adolescents live in a predominantly secular and/or Christian society. "God" is the subject of numerous jokes, a few decent movies, and a lot of "faithful" Christian proclamations of uncritical belief. Rarely is "God" the subject of thoughtful reflection.

The challenge of the Holocaust to faith in God could, if handled improperly, simply confirm Jewish teenagers in their theological indifference. Any program on the Holocaust has to help build an understanding of various Jewish concepts of God as well as challenge those conceptions in the name of the Holocaust. I wanted students to leave the simulation somewhat awed at the richness and depth of Jewish thinking about God. If these resources were ultimately unable to meet the challenge of the Holocaust, I wanted Jewish teenagers to attribute the failure to the magnitude of the event. I did not want to confirm—even indirectly—the conventional wisdom that belief in God is an unimportant aspect of our Jewishness.

4. Finally, the resources of Jewish theology had to be selected carefully. I wanted to transmit the diversity of different responses to tragedy implicit in various theological positions. For myself, this meant steering away from some of the most contemporary interpretations of the Holocaust. These approaches either take for granted or radically transvalue some of the basic assumptions of Jewish theology (e.g., God cares about human beings,

divine-human communication is possible, etc.). For Jewish teenagers unschooled in "Godtalk," the theologies of Richard Rubenstein, Emil Fackenheim, and Eliezer Berkowitz are literally baseless. I wanted to choose four Jewish thinkers whose thinking reflected, as clearly as possible, rudimentary theological positions.

The Kallah

I began my section of the *kallah* (one and a half hours; subsequent experience has shown that this is too long for Jewish teenagers and not long enough for adults) by explaining what I wanted to accomplish in our time together. I shared with the participants my personal feeling that one could not really talk about God and the Holocaust without first focusing on some of the ideas about God we had already developed as individuals. I then asked if anyone had thought about God in the past week. Only a few people raised their hands. The next question was whether individuals felt that there was a God. Almost everyone raised a hand.

The final introductory question was obvious: Why the difference in response to these first two questions? If so many of us felt that there is a God, why did so few of us think about God in the past week? I encouraged students to explain the apparent absence of "God" in our week. Several pointed out that "God" might be apparent in our actions (if we did a mitzvah), even if not in our thoughts. My suggestion to the participants was that we most often turn to God in times of a disaster. We think about the meaning of God in our life when someone in the family dies, when disease threatens our own life, or when a great tragedy—like the Holocaust—affects the Jewish people.

I went on to explain that this afternoon we wanted to try to begin our discussion about God on a non-tragic note. Today was Shabbat. Tradition has it that each Jew has a *neshamah yeterah*, an additional soul, on Shabbat. Out of our beautiful ceremonies, rest, and friendships, came a special sensitivity. I asked the participants to rely on that extra sensitivity as I read through a list of God-beliefs (see Appendix A). Their task was not to analyze but simply to relax and allow their own inner, spiritual selves to respond to whether each statement contained a God-belief they held. I expressed my hope that each of them would at some point in their lives (if not this weekend) be able to give some serious thought to each of the statements. (When the program is not held on Shabbat, it helps to have participants actually check off their answers on a copy sheet. Preliminary music and sensory relaxation techniques might also be of some help in a different context.)

Personal Beliefs and the Holocaust

I next asked the participants to imagine the following: They themselves had survived the Holocaust but had lost their families in a concentration camp. The God-beliefs sheet was then passed out to each of the participants. Everyone was asked to read over the sheet. This time the perspective was not their own personal beliefs, but how they thought they would respond to each God-belief with such vivid memories of the Holocaust coloring their perspective.

This particular group of students handled the task extremely well. While understanding that some individuals might emerge from the experience with God-beliefs unaltered (or even paradoxically strengthened), they immediately recognized that certain beliefs were directly contradicted by the events of the Holocaust. Surely, they reasoned, a God who *could* answer prayer *would* have answered the desperate prayers of the Jews who perished in the Holocaust (belief #5). Other beliefs, like #1 (God directs the happenings in the world), were challenged on the grounds that they were implicitly discredited by the Holocaust. God could have directed the events leading up to the Holocaust, but then he could not be called a "good" God, as indicated in another statement. Some students began to understand some of the even more complex interrelationships between the beliefs. If one believes, for instance, that God intended us never to understand certain things about the world (#7), then one could still believe that God directed the events in the world (#1), or that God's goodness was of a different order than human beings could understand.

At this point in the program, the leader's role is twofold. First, the leader needs to decide at what level s/he would like the discussion to continue. My own sense is that the discussion merited several hours of class time outside of the *kallah*. Sophisticated work has been done by Ellen Charry playing (in an almost mathematical way) with the various permutations and clusters of God-beliefs and their relationships to the four theological positions presented later.[1] For the immediate purposes of the *kallah*, however, the discussion needed to end on an inconclusive note.

Second, the leader serves an important function in providing more comprehensive Jewish contexts for evaluating the various God statements. It is possible, for instance, that God intends certain things to be beyond our comprehension. The leader, however, needs to point out that Jews have always stubbornly held that through the Torah there is a standard of goodness in the world to which even God is accountable. And if these words produce too casual a nod from the participants, the leader needs

---

1. Available through the Curriculum Resource Center of Gratz College, Philadelphia, Pennsylvania.

to provide a more complete and more balanced picture through reference to the Book of Job.

The discussion section of the *kallah* focusing on God-beliefs came to a close after fifteen to twenty minutes of discussion. We tried to effect some closure by asking ourselves how many of the God-beliefs might have to be scrapped if one took seriously the religious and moral implications of the Holocaust. After a brief polling, it was decided that at least thirteen of the twenty-one beliefs listed would have to be abandoned or radically modified.

What, then, does one do with the shredded fabric of Jewish faith in God after the Holocaust? I tried to place the event in the context of Jewish and Zionist history. Indeed, precisely because of events like the Holocaust, many sensitive Jews had decided that Judaism had to function through commitments to the land of Israel rather than to the God of Israel, to the "traditions" rather than the "theology" of the Jewish people, and to the "culture" rather than the "religion" of classical Judaism. I shared with them my deep respect for this kind of commitment to Judaism and the Jewish people. I took a few moments to explain how my own attachment to Judaism had been shaped largely through my experience in Israel rather than through theological beliefs.

Yet "God" has a long and honored history in the Jewish tradition. The Jewish tradition itself was in many ways forged in response to tragedy. Perhaps there were, I suggested, ways of retaining a deep personal belief in God even after the Holocaust. At any rate, I indicated that I would like to explore with them the positions of four outstanding Jewish thinkers who felt that belief in God could be sustained even in the face of tragedy.

Encounter with Four Jewish Thinkers

The goal of the encounter was to provide students with an opportunity to interact with the personalities and thoughts of four significant Jewish thinkers. The element of drama was fostered by having each of the thinkers visit the *kallah* and challenge the view that the Holocaust destroyed faith in God. Each thinker tried to present his theological position through concrete situations which were part of the students' everyday life. The students were asked to listen to all four thinkers and to respond to each as a survivor of the Holocaust. After all four had made their visits, participants would be given the opportunity to call any of the thinkers back and challenge what they had said. All challenges, however, had to be in the form of dialogue. One had to talk to Jeremiah, Gersonides, Elie Wiesel, or Mordecai Kaplan. Participants could not simply talk about their beliefs. The dramatic and dialogic nature of the encounters were crucial if the theological beliefs were to remain comprehensible to early adolescents. The foundations of and some useful techniques for such an approach to role-playing have been well documented by Viola Spolin.[2]

Conceptual clarity and simplicity were also important. Each thinker based his presentation on a single phrase. As the thinker came forward, he displayed a placard with the phrase in both Hebrew and English. During the course of the presentation, reference was made in a visual way by pointing to the card (sometimes more than once). The four thinkers and their placards were:

Jeremiah:
Mipney Hata'enu Galinu Me-artzeynu
(Because of our sins we were exiled from our land)

Gersonides:
Ain Hashgahah Peratit
(God does not govern the particular details of our lives)

Elie Wiesel:
Shitufim im Elohim be-Ma'aseh Bereshit
(We are partners with God in maintaining the Creation)

Mordecai Kaplan:
Tzedek, Tzedek, Tirdof
(Justice, justice shall you pursue)

In general, one can say the following of the four thinkers. Jeremiah is broadly representative of the "traditionalist" response to tragedy, Gersonides of the "rationalist" response, Wiesel of the "mystical" approach, and Kaplan of the "naturalist" response.

While these thinkers vary considerably in the depth of their philosophical thinking, they all try to "make sense of" and "think about" the significance of tragedy in ways that Green[3] and others have suggested is the hallmark of modern, analytic philosophy. The list of Jewish thinkers who have other approaches to the problems of suffering and theodicy is long. Eugene Borowitz's *Choices in Modern Jewish Thought* (Behrman House, 1983) is a particularly rich resource that can be used to construct other simulations. (Note especially his chapter "Confronting the Holocaust" [pp. 185-218] for this purpose. The positions of such thinkers

---

2. Viola Spolin, *Improvisation for the Theater*. (Evanston: Northwestern University Press, 1963.)
3. Thomas Green, *The Activities of Teaching*. (McGraw Hill, 1971), 9-14.

as Fackenheim, Berkovitz, and Jonas, outlined in this chapter, might be examined for their elements of continuity and discontinuity with the most basic Jewish responses.)

My experience now tells me that using all four characters is an overload on what most participants (teenage and adult) can process. I suggest choosing the three positions with which the individual (or individuals, if a staff is working together on the simulation) is most comfortable (both dramatically and theologically). For reasons I don't completely understand (perhaps it is an idiosyncratic presentation of Wiesel), Kaplan's and Wiesel's positions tend to coalesce in the minds of the participants.

Of the four thinkers, I was personally least familiar with Gersonides. Reading about his life and thought in *Encyclopedia Judaica* and in Husik's *A History of Medieval Jewish Philosophy* was extremely useful. For Jeremiah, I reread the Book of Jeremiah and skimmed over sections of John Skinner's *Prophecy and Religion* (which deals with the life and thought of Jeremiah). I felt sufficiently familiar with the thought of Elie Wiesel and Mordecai Kaplan to present each spontaneously. The key in all instances is for the leader to feel comfortable with the core theological concept s/he is presenting. Wider and deeper exposure to each thinker helps free the leader to be more spontaneous in his interactions with the participants. Such mastery may point to the wisdom of working on the simulation as a staff, so that each individual can involve himself in greater depth with the life and thought of one of the thinkers. The overall goal of the simulation, however, should always be kept in mind. The goal is not to conduct a graduate seminar in theology. An hour or so of study for each character is probably sufficient for most teachers. (The dramatic ability of the leader[s] is, of course, variable, but I can assure everyone that this writer has no great or hidden talent in this area. Any teacher who can do role-plays in a classroom can fit into the presentations.)

What follows is a brief sketch of the presentations made by each of the four thinkers. As characters entered, students were asked to treat each as a guest. They would be given an opportunity to call back the thinkers in order to challenge their positions. Meanwhile, they would have to judge for themselves about the adequacy of each position as a theological solution to the problem of Jewish faith in God after the Holocaust.

Jeremiah (The Traditionalist Response)

> Shalom. My name is Jeremiah. I am one of the Hebrew prophets of old. I come to visit you because I want you to know that your questions are not new. You are not the first group of Jews who have encountered suffering

and despair. You are not the first group whose sins were punished by the God of Israel.

It happened in my day, too. People were wailing in the streets. The leaders of the Jewish people had been exiled to Babylonia. The Temple had been destroyed. Nobody could figure out why this had happened. What had we done to deserve such a fate?

Why were we punished? I nearly laughed in their faces. Do you know what went on back then? Everyone had deserted God and His covenant. The priests of the time cared about nothing so much as their own power. Do you think it bothered them if the people on the hillside had to become poor in order to support the priests and the Temple? And I want you to know that the poor, common people were no great bargain, either. What did they put their trust in? It was all the rage in my day to have a figurine of Astarte, the Egyptian Goddess.

Why were they punished? Idolatry! Immorality! Deserting the Covenant! I used to tell my wailing countrymen that the real miracle was not that they had been punished, but that God would, in time, return hope to Zion and restore the Jewish poeple to their land.

Do you see the sign I brought with me? Do you see what it says? That's right—*Mipney Hata'enu Galinu Me-artzeynu*, because of our sins were we exiled. Tradition credits me with having written that verse. You can find it in the Book of Lamentations. In fact, I don't even remember if I wrote it at all. It's all really very simple. God makes demands of us. If we cannot live up to these demands, there is punishment. It's part of the Covenant with the Jewish people. Everyone is accountable for his actions.

It's as true for you as it was for me...and for the Jews who perished in the Holocaust. How many of you are so righteous? How many of you have never cheated on an exam to get a good grade? Lied to a friend to impress him with an accomplishment you never did?

Wait—just a second—How many of you really observe the Sabbath? I know you do it here, but I mean in your homes. Do you have a Sabbath or a Saturday, watch television or go to synagogue?

Do you think God sees all these flaws in your character and just says, "Ho-hum, another straying Israelite." If there was no punishment for wrong-doing there would be no Covenant. I don't pretend to know why each and every Jew in the Holocaust died. But I do know that God holds us account-able for our wrongdoings. And I know that man does a lot that is wrong. Somehow even the Holocaust was just and fair. Because of our sins, all these tragedies happen to the Jewish people.

Gersonides (The Rationalist Response)

Shalom. I am Levi Ben Gerson. Perhaps only a few of you know me, simply because you have not yet taken the right courses in the history of astronomy and Jewish philosophy. I belong in both. I was a great astronomer of the fourteenth century (learned Christians invited me to their courts to instruct them in the sciences) and a pious and knowledgeable Jew.

I understand that you are troubled by the problem of human suffering, the problem of why so many Jews died in—what do you call it?—oh yes, the Holocaust.

The people in my generation were troubled by this problem too. Many of my fellow rabbis would spend hours trying to console Jews when a young child would die, or trying to explain to an honest, God-fearing Jew why he was still so poor. Why had not God repaid him for his devotion to the Torah? Yes, people were very troubled by this question. But I was always able to give them the simplest of answers. It is the same one that I offer you.

God is not concerned with what happens to each of us as individuals. This is left to us, to our free wills, to the kind of life we live, and to the kinds of communities we create.

God, oh, the egotism of Your creatures! Do you really think that your everyday concerns matter to God? Do you really think He cares that your stomachs are growling in protest against camp food? Does it matter to God whether or not the boy or girl you would like to become more friendly with smiled at you at lunch? Is it important for God to be with you in your time of distress—like when you get a small scoop at the ice cream parlor and are clearly cheated?

There are two things I always do with people who are looking for an answer to this question of why the righteous suffer. First, I always take them with me to look out at the stars and ask, "Is not the God who created such beauty as these too great and distant to be concerned about your individual problems? Isn't it enough to just look up and know that you are part of God's miraculous creation? Doesn't some of your suffering go away when you feel so small under the sky?"

Then I tell my friends that God's plan is the following: He does not come down to us; we climb up to Him. We must elevate ourselves, our character. We must come to see the world as God sees it. Then we will all know how to do justice to one another, then there will be no more tragedies.

Ain Hashgahah Peratit—God does not concern Himself with the everyday details of our life. If He were to help us every time we cried or did not understand something, we would not grow into the wise creatures He intends us to be. God gives us the power to do the good and understand the world. If He interfered with our human abilities to do those things, He would be violating His own plan for the world.

Elie Wiesel (The Mystical Approach)

I've come to share some thoughts with you about the Holocaust. And you see, unlike your last two guests, I speak from experience. For I am a survivor of the Holocaust. My whole life has been shaped by that horrible event. Every word I write is touched by it.

It used to be that I was the angriest of men. I lost my whole family in the Holocaust. The very thought of the event created indescribable anguish inside of me. I was a storyteller then as now. But the only story I could tell was that of Rabbi Levi of Berditchev. Do you know of Rabbi Levi? He was a great Hasidic rabbi.

The tale goes like this. During Yom Kippur, Rabbi Levi of Berditchev excused himself from services. He went outside and made a personal petition of God. He said:

> Master of the Universe, in there—in the *shul*—I ask You for Your forgiveness. Surely I have sinned. But Master of the Universe, You sin even more. Think of all the unjustified and horrible suffering which has come upon the Jewish people. Surely there is no good reason for this. Surely it is in Your power to stop it.
>
> So, Master of the Universe, I have a deal to make with You. I have here two lists. One is a list of the sins which my people have committed against You. The other is a list of Your sins against them. I think You know whose list is longer.
>
> But You teach me to be compassionate as You Yourself are compassionate. So I will make a deal with You. If you will forgive the Jewish people for their sins against You, I will forgive You for Your transgressions against them.

Yes, for many years this was the only story that I could tell. But times have changed now. I don't feel so bitter. I no longer hold God accountable for the Holocaust. Perhaps, after all, He was powerless to stop it. My thoughts turn now to that loveliest and most intriguing idea, taken from the great commentaries on the Book of Genesis. There we are told that You and I, God, are *shitufim*, partners, in the act of creation.

I believe that, and so I believe that God is waiting for us to do something about our part of the world. One ancient mystic suggested that God's relation to man and to the world might be compared to a person locked up in prison. God waits for man to perform just the right good deed which will unlock the door and make the world a fit place—as it must have been once—for God's presence to dwell in. Yes, when we really do become partners with God in creating a new world, perhaps the nightmare of the Holocaust will leave me for good.

Mordecai Kaplan (The Naturalist Response)

You know that all my life I have been teaching *Kol Yisrael Arevim Zeh Lazeh*, each and every Jew is responsible for the welfare of all other Jews. So of course the Holocaust is very painful for me. If I am a member of the great Jewish family, then I can't escape the fact that over one-third of my family was murdered during the Holocaust. Even if I had not lost members of my real family, I would have felt the sting no less.

So why, people ask me, do I still have faith in man and God? Perhaps part of it is that I am an optimist. When the siddur tells us that "each day the work of creation is renewed," I believe it. I believe that each day is full of new opportunities for living the kind of life described in the Torah—a good life, a religious life, a moral life.

Each of us has the power to pursue justice. The Book of Deuteronomy says it clearly: *"Tzedek Tzedek Tirdof'* – justice, justice shall you pursue. Why does it say justice twice in the Torah? There are many explanations given. My own is that *tzedek* is written twice to teach us that part of our ability to do justice comes from the power in the world we call God. One *tzedek* is ours; the other is His. Together we have the capacity to change the world for the better.

Not everyone takes advantage of this gift. If everyone did, we would never have Holocausts. But a hundred Holocausts cannot erase the privilege each of us is granted each day in awakening to the potential of making the world a better place.

Follow-Up and Evaluation of Program

After presenting the four thinkers, the participants are encouraged to call back individuals and challenge their views. My experience with various groups is that Jeremiah is almost always called back quickly. Participants challenge his notion that all punishment is just, in the name of innocent children who perished in the Holocaust. Surely, they did not live long enough to have sinned in such a way as to bring down God's wrath. Sometimes this leads to a quite long and extended trek through the notion of corporate responsibility in the Bible, and sometimes Jeremiah is defeated quickly. Gersonides' somewhat dispassionate attitude is usually either amusing or mildly disturbing to different groups. Only sophisticated groups of adults call back Mordecai Kaplan or Elie Wiesel for questioning.

After extending the questions and answers for whatever time is deemed appropriate, the mask of theater is dropped. Individuals are asked which of the four positions comes closest to approximating their own. With adequate time, small group discussions of how the program affected the participants and the reasons for their final choices can provide closure.

My experiences have been largely successful in the various settings in which I have used this program. As I look back over why I chose this particular approach, I realize how deeply impressed I must have been with the story of the University of California at Berkeley professor who used to teach his history of science class by coming to class dressed as the scientist to be discussed each week. Theology is too important to remain an activity solely for theologians. When concepts are simplified and embodied in a living person, theology can come alive for Jewish teenagers and adults.

Appendix: GOD-BELIEFS*

1) I believe that God created the world and directs the happenings in it.
2) I believe that God has no power to interfere in the affairs of people.
3) I believe that the world came into being by accident.
4) I believe that God is aware of what I do.
5) I believe that God can answer prayer.
6) I believe that God punishes evil.
7) I believe that God intended us never to understand certain things about the world.
8) I believe that my concepts about God differ from the Torah's concept of God.
9) I believe that even if there were no people, God would still exist.
10) I believe that God decided what is good and what is evil.
11) I believe that God gets involved in human affairs when God wants to.
12) I believe that God rewards good.
13) I believe that God exists independently of, and outside of people.
14) I believe that prayer is an attempt to talk to God.
15) I believe that the Torah is the word of God.
16) I believe that God listens to prayer.
17) I believe that "God" is a term that people use to describe their best hopes for humanity.
18) I believe God exists only inside of people.
19) I believe that praying can benefit the person who prays, even if God doesn't listen.
20) I believe that "God" is an idea people use to describe those things beyond human understanding.
21) I believe prayer can have an effect on people's lives regardless of what they think about God.

---

* From *Cookbook of Jewish Ideas* by Ellen Charry (Philadelphia: Bureau of Jewish Education of Philadelphia).

Reconstructing Teachers and Curricula*

■ ■ ■ Sidney H. Schwarz

In the flawed system of imparting Jewish education which we call Hebrew school, not the least of our problems is finding competent teachers. Part of the growing pains of a developing Reconstructionist congregation is the particular problem of finding teachers who are not only competent, but also able to teach Judaism to our children from a Reconstructionist perspective. Since there is neither a Reconstructionist network of teacher training nor a youth movement, the pickings are slim. Most synagogues have no choice but to find the best teachers and to train them themselves, so that there can be some consistency between what the rabbi and adult congregants believe and what is being taught to the children. These comments are intended as a guide for a series of workshops aimed at meeting this need.

It should be pointed out that this does not address the need for the restructuring of our entire curriculum to reflect more fully the broad spectrum of Reconstructionism's approach to Jewish civilization. We need to develop materials appropriate to the primary level which deal with Jewish art and literature and the products of modern Hebrew culture from Israel. But short of that, the standard fare of our Hebrew schools can also better reflect a Reconstructionist understanding of Judaism.

It cannot be expected that all of our teachers will agree with all aspects of Reconstructionist philosophy. In fact, indoctrination of either teachers

---

* An earlier version of this essay appeared in *Reconstructionist*, October 1981.

or students should not be our goal. The presentation of the basic concepts of Reconstructionism can be well integrated into the normal course
of a school curriculum and should serve to broaden the horizons of
thought and inquiry for the students without attaching any labels to the
ideas. The presentation of Reconstructionism as a systematic ideology of
Jewish life is probably better left for a post-bar mitzvah-level class.
However, an understanding by teachers of some basic Reconstructionist
approaches to the five areas listed below can aid the educational process
considerably.

God

Teachers should stress that Judaism allows for a variety of God ideas.
All too often, a child is presented with a supernatural God concept in
the context of a miraculous Bible story and never hears God spoken about
in any other way. When that child comes to question that concept of God,
he feels as if he has betrayed a basic tenet of Judaism. Many of my
brightest students have told me that they are atheists, not knowing that
their theological doubts were only the beginning of an exciting search
for religious truths. Our loss of a significant number of bright Jewish
teenagers is due, in part, to the failure of our teachers and curricula to
explore questions of God in a thoughtful and sophisticated manner.

Just as we must be sure to present children at the earliest ages with
ideas of God that go beyond the "supernatural grandfather in heaven,"
so we must be careful not to ridicule the children who still find such a
conception believable. As crucial as the presentation of new, challenging
God ideas is the process by which students learn to understand and
tolerate views that they themselves do not hold. This applies to all areas
of Jewish education.

The most sophisticated theologies can be reduced to easily understandable ideas for the Hebrew school level. Finite vs. infinite God, supernatural vs. natural, transcendent and existentialist approaches are all ideas
that children think about but generally lack the language to express. These
theologies can and must be placed in their language and be presented
as equally valid theological options.

An excellent graphic of different theologies in easy language appears
in *Shema is for Real!* by Joel Grishaver.[1] There, Grishaver uses the image
of a puppet-master to illustrate the concept of a supernatural God. He
uses a watchmaker who makes a watch, winds it up and then leaves it
running to explicate the idea of a finite God. We have used this approach

---

1. Joel Grishaver, *Shema is for Real!* (Chicago: Olin-Sang Ruby Institute, UAHC, 1973), 77.

successfully with ten-year-olds. More important than the theological labels has been the fact that God-models have been offered with which the students could identify.

Reconstructionist theology is eagerly discussed in the primary grade classroom. Kaplan's assertions about the nature of the universe invite the question of whether the world is good, evil, or neutral. Put differently: Is good or evil more natural to our world, and what are the consequences of believing one way or the other? Harold Schulweis' predicate theology is easily adapted into exercises for students.[2] Each child lists those human qualities that make for morality or the betterment of the world. A teacher can then point out how these qualities were personified into the God idea by our ancestors. A discussion can ensue about how we can speak of God as a role model for ourselves (*imitatio dei*).

Finally teachers should be encouraged to read Harold Kushner's *When Children Ask About God* (Reconstructionist Press, 1971).

Bible

A teacher of mine used to say that the Bible is not great because it is divine; it is divine because it is great. It is amazing how in some of our most progressive synagogues the Bible is taught in a way that resembles the way in which it might be taught in a fundamentalist church. We do no greater injustice to the minds of our children than to tell them "Bible stories." While we hope that in future years students will probe more deeply into the significance of the Bible, this is no excuse for leaving students with a series of nonsensical associations with the classic biblical stories. For example, Noah: God sent a flood and Noah built an ark; the *Akedah*: God wanted Abraham to sacrifice his son, and Abraham stood willing until God changed his mind; the Red Sea: Moses and Israel escaped the pursuing Egyptians by miraculously passing through the sea, which then closed and drowned the Egyptians.

We must insist that teachers pose basic questions in any presentation of Bible stories. I suggest the following: 1) What is the moral of the story? 2) What do you think really happened? 3) Why was the story told this way? I have found that students only begin to understand the Bible when the narratives are naturalized. That is to say, when students read a biblical story and disregard the active role attributed to God by the narrator, they are forced to come to grips with the way in which biblical personalities actually acted. Since students can rarely conceive of God

---

2. See Harold Schulweis, "From God to Godliness: Proposal for a Predicate Theology," *Reconstructionist* 41 (February, 1975): 16-26.

speaking to them, it is helpful to examine the actions of a biblical character and then to discuss why that character might have thought that God would have wanted him to act in such a way. Students then find it easier to discuss and evaluate biblical stories because a teacher can indicate how we make choices in our own lives based on what we feel we ought to do.

As one example, let us look at what happens when we naturalize the biblical account of the *Akedah*. Abraham's actions can no longer be explained by saying that he was merely obeying God's command or that the sacrifice was prevented due to the intercession of an angel. By eliminating the supernatural layer of the story, many questions are invited. Where did Abraham get the idea of sacrificing his son? How could he have believed that this was what God wanted? Why didn't Sarah and Isaac have any say in the matter? Is it possible to misunderstand "God's voice"? How and why did Abraham come to change his mind? Can we commit ourselves to principles but remain open to changes of heart? The questions, of course, can go on. I often like to reintroduce God into the discussion at the end as the pervasive factor throughout the story that seems to affect peoples' thoughts and actions in a way that makes them look beyond their self-centered concerns. I like the students to apply these associations to the role which God plays in their own lives as well.

This does not mean that we must rewrite the Bible, excising all miracles and supernatural events. Quite the contrary. Such accounts allow us to understand the way our ancestors perceived their own history. It is important that our children appreciate that basic to ancient Jewish theology was the belief in God's power of salvation, particularly with regard to the Jewish people. We cannot know what happened at the Red Sea any more than we can know what happened at Sinai. Some students will find the miraculous accounts palatable, others will not. We do know, however, that the Jewish people interpreted those events as evidence of a supernatural God whose concern was especially for them. It is healthy to engage our students in a discussion as to whether they subscribe to biblical theology at the same time as the point is made that our religious beliefs have evolved over time. Finally, a distinction needs to be made that the Bible is not intended as history but as a theological interpretation of history, and that interpretation has been subject to successive generations of religious genius and reinterpretation.

A good treatment of how one goes beyond the theological language of the Bible to its values is Ronald Brauner's "Values in the Bible."[3]

---

3. Ronald Brauner, "Values in the Bible," *Pedagogic Reporter* 30 (Spring, 1979): 2-5.

Prayer

Most curricula give scant attention to prayer beyond rote recitation. This usually reflects difficulties that teachers themselves have with prayer, and this problem can be compounded in light of a non-supernatural theology. Teachers can be offered four purposes of prayer that usually aid in presentation to students. They involve seeing prayer as: an expression of our fears and hopes; the expression of the sense of wonder at and appreciation of the world around us; the articulation of our values; and a link to generations of Jews of the past as well as to Jews living all over the world today.

Students may be asked to take the traditional liturgy and label each prayer in one of these four categories. More categories may be created and many prayers may fall into a number of the groups. Another exercise which aids in understanding prayer is to follow the lead of the *Reconstructionist Sabbath Prayer Book*[4] in the way it offers interpretive versions of traditional prayers. Promoting maximal latitude, teachers can encourage students to write their own interpretive versions of prayers whose language may be problematic for them.

Holidays

Our school would score a major achievement if we succeeded in having the students recount the ethical as the primary association with each holiday instead of the miraculous. Kaplan, in *The Meaning of God in Modern Jewish Religion*,[5] calls this the process of "revaluation." It involves the sifting out from traditional religious ideas and institutions of those elements which are rooted in an ancient world view and to which we no longer subscribe. While leaving these elements aside, we retain and emphasize those elements which reflect ongoing values and concerns of man and society. Ira Eisenstein's *What We Mean By Religion* (Reconstructionist Press) provides such an interpretation of the holidays suitable for classroom use.

Many schools, however, do not tackle holidays as a major part of the curriculum each year. Instead, most students gain impressions of holidays from the half-hour lesson immediately prior to a festival. It is important for principals to provide teachers with a mini-guide just for these quick

---

4. *Reconstructionist Sabbath Prayer Book* (New York: Jewish Reconstructionist Foundation, 1945).
5. Mordecai M. Kaplan, *The Meaning of God in Modern Jewish Religion* (New York: Reconstructionist Press, 1964).

lessons on holidays. Left to their own devices, many teachers will present students with a fairy-tale version of the holiday that they themselves learned as children. Ideally, teachers should be provided with a graded lesson plan that presents the holidays thematically and indicates the major values that are at the core of each. Students should then be encouraged to marshal current events and their own life experiences to illustrate the universal and particular dimensions of the holiday's lessons.

A discussion of Hanukah, for example, as the festival of religious liberty and conscience should get students to be aware of religious persecution in the world. They might be asked if they can think of an ideal that is worth dying for. Perhaps they can consider whether the freedom of our society makes us take religion for granted. Pesah provides the opportunity to consider the tyranny and oppression in the world and the value of human freedom. What are the limits of dissent or civil disobedience when authority is abused? What are the Jewish models for standing up in the face of political injustice? On Shavuot, teachers might talk about the centrality of Torah to Judaism and about the role of law in society. Students might be asked to compare morality, justice, and law and to consider why these terms are not always synonymous. They might also be asked to think about whether law limits or allows for freedom.

Some excellent values lessons on holidays appear in *There is a Season*, published by Alternatives in Religious Education.[6]

Chosenness

Even though Kaplan's rejection of the notion and language of Jewish chosenness is one of his less popular positions, his concern that ethnocentrism is at the root of much societal discord remains a warning and a lesson very much worth teaching. Unfortunately, in our desire to give our students a shield of Jewish pride as protection in a sometimes hostile world, we commit grave errors of religious/ethnic chauvinism. I am astounded at how many of our children tell me that Jews are better than non-Jews. Wherever they received that notion, I feel that our school has failed if it does not disabuse them of the idea.

There are many subtle ways that we give children the impression that non-Jews are bad or that they are less religious and ethical than we are. This often is the hidden message students get when they learn about anti-Semitism or the Holocaust. The issue is one that must be brought out

---

6. *There is a Season: A Values Clarification Approach to Jewish Holidays* (Denver: Alternatives in Religious Education, 1973).

into the open lest the students develop their own harmful prejudices. The causes of hatred and intolerance are social pathologies; they are not genetic. We must understand such pathologies as well as possible and do all we can to root them out of our societies. Adopting our own defensive hatreds is most certainly no solution.

Teachers should also point out the dangers of certain religious teachings that breed chauvinism. Many children have heard from their parents or teachers that religion is the root of intolerance and war in today's world, as it has been throughout history. Certainly there is much to bear out such a claim on the news programs we watch every evening. Our schools must confront this challenge to religion by demonstrating that there is good religion and bad religion. We should point out the teachings within Christianity, Islam, and Judaism that have bred chauvinism and intolerance. At the same time, teachers can show how religions can transcend their own doctrines so as to make themselves forces for justice and morality in the world.

In an open, pluralistic society it is important for us to teach our children that all religions are attempts to aid human beings to fulfill themselves spiritually and morally. Each religion in its own way has given a particular form to its conception of the world and, in the process, has laid claims to some exclusive possession of Truth. If history has taught us anything, it is that no one religion has ever cornered the market on truth, and that each has a long way to go before it approximates the greater truth.

In a world filled with religious zealots who place more effort in marketing their faulty wares than in perfecting their product, we would do well to impart to our children a message of religious pluralism. Our children do not have to be told that Judaism is the best religion in the world to turn back a missionary with a simple "Live and let live." Finally, if our Hebrew school curricula leave our children with a sense that the purpose of religion generally is to make our lives more meaningful and the world a better place to live, instead of leaving them with memories of juvenile fairy tales, we may stand a chance of getting those children back into our synagogues when they grow up.

On Teaching the Holocaust*

■ ■ ■ David Blumenthal

An interesting statistic surfaced in a recent conversation with a colleague from psychology: in courses which are not related to a student's major, ninety-two percent of the material will be forgotten within three months of the final examination or paper. This evidence should lead us to reflect on the purpose of instruction in the humanities in general. In connection with the teaching of the Holocaust, the issue raised by this statistic is even more poignant because the material itself has a morally pressing quality about it. In an attempt to respond to this situation, I propose that there are two ways for scholars to teach the Holocaust, both of which can yield substantial results.

The first way of teaching the Holocaust is to regard it as a subject for research, just as we regard any other area of human endeavor as a subject of research. This we can call the "scholarly" approach, and the number of men and women who have devoted their energies to researching this period is legion. Books continue to multiply and the number of detailed studies of this or that aspect or incident continues to increase. We are rapidly reaching the point where no one can read all the literature in the field, and I suppose this means that "Holocaust Studies" has come of age.

Within the scholarly world, however, there appear to be major differences of interpretation, major variations in hermeneutic stance.[1] Thus, some scholars propose that the Holocaust can be studied only in its very

---

* Reprinted from *Reconstructionist*, April 1980.
1. I have tried to sort out this complicated issue in "Scholarly Approaches to the Holocaust," *Sho'ah* 1 (Winter, 1979) 21-27.

specific context and that no trans-contextual, general forces were at work. The Holocaust, according to this way of thinking, is the sum of its very specific parts; no more. Other scholars propose that the Holocaust was a product of general forces at work in modern society – forces which were not unique to the situation of Germany in the years of the Holocaust. Totalitarianism, bureaucratization, fascism, volkism, charismatic leadership, anti-Semitism, etc. have been variously identified as the forces which were present in Holocaust Germany, which were not unique to it and which, from a scholarly point of view, "created" or "caused" the Holocaust. At stake here seems to be the question, "Is history the sum of its moments, each defined by a specific context, or is history the product of general forces at work in society of which the specific events are but a manifestation?" To teach the Holocaust in this way is, then, to pose exactly that question, the question of the nature of historical knowledge. It is, then, to confront the opposing, or rather varying, interpretive stances to the data and, then, to let the students fight it out for themselves. In using this approach, the teacher need not treat the Holocaust as different from any other period of history. It is enough to pose the broad question and then the various interpretive stances.

A variant on this scholarly approach to teaching the Holocaust is to take one of the interpretive stances, examine its theses, and then test them against the evidence. One could take Nolte's thesis which, if I understand it correctly, states that it was Hitler's personality which radicalized good old-fashioned middle European conservatives, and then seek out the evidence to test it. Or, one could take Rubenstein's insights into the nature of the rationalization of society through bureaucracy and labor policies, and seek out the evidence to test that hypothesis.[2] In using this approach, the teacher must force students to recognize a hypothesis when one is offered, and to learn how to test it against the evidence. The student has to learn how to judge, how to take sides in a scholarly debate. Here, too, however, the Holocaust period need not be treated differently from any other historical period. It is a question of method within history. The material may be repulsive, but one must overcome that; one must bracket the rage, as Rubenstein has said.

I want, however, to make a plea for the legitimacy of a completely different approach to the teaching of the Holocaust. Let us call it what it is: "non-scholarly." I realize that I offend my scholarly colleagues in Holocaust Studies even with the suggestion, and I admit that I would not warmly welcome the proposal that colleagues start teaching Jewish mysticism and philosophy, which are my fields, in a "non-scholarly" way.

---

2. Ibid., esp. 21-23.

What distinguishes the university is that it is a scholarly enterprise, a learned seeking after detailed orderly knowledge. Nonetheless, with a genuine acknowledgement of my inadequacies, I think I represent a relatively large class of university faculty who, for various reasons, have rejected the period of the Holocaust as the major focus of their scholarly research, yet who feel compelled to deal with this material. Let me note at the outset that I do not teach the Holocaust in order to generate enrollment. It is not the most popular course I teach. It is, on the other hand, the most emotionally difficult course I teach. It attracts the most irregular students on campus and provokes the most emotional reactions. I would give it up, if I could.

What, then, possesses a person who is a scholar in his/her own area to venture, in a non-scholarly way, into a difficult and unknown domain? Or, to put it another way: Why should the non-scholar in the Holocaust teach the material altogether? Is there room for such a course in a university? The answers to these questions will determine what it is that one wants to teach; that is, the answer to the question "Why teach?" will generate the material for the course.

The response of each of us who teaches the Holocaust in a non-scholarly way is different. I can only speak for myself. There are three reasons why I teach the Holocaust. First, my motivation stems from recurrent dialogic confrontation with survivors. I heard Simon Wiesenthal tell us that he was not the Jewish James Bond but an old Jew with a heart condition who, when he came out of the camps, had to believe in something. I saw my great uncle's tattoo; I wear his pocket watch; my son bears his name. I see the courage on the faces of the survivors who come to class and drag up all the humiliation and rage. I see the films, and I am ashamed of my compensatory fantasies which are clearly intended to soften what my eyes have seen. The most difficult part of being human is simply standing vis-à-vis the other, being present and not fleeing the other's presence. And, as I stand over against the survivors, I know I must try to teach the material.

Second, as I try to be present to the survivors, I also try to be present to the students. It is easy to convey information, even if students will forget ninety-two percent of it. It is relatively easy to convey the scholarly problematic that stands behind the information. It is, however, very difficult to be present to students, to stand and to let them look into your eyes. I don't think I am disproportionately neurotic, but I find presentness more difficult than scholarship. As I look at students today, I find that some of them (not all) need this element of personal dialogic presence. And they need it most in material which is difficult to bear. They need it most with material that is upsetting, that is deeply bound to their image of themselves, of society, and of mankind. The Holocaust did happen and students (indeed almost all people), when they confront the data of the Holocaust, with all of its violence, with all of the repressed feelings which it brings to the surface, require a standing vis-à-vis by the teacher. And, as I stand over against the students, I know I must try to teach the material.

Third, the record of academics during the Holocaust is nothing to brag about. In fact, it is repulsively ugly. Men and women with the best that European culture and education could give them turned sadist, sold their moral integrity, and in their "finest" moments, remained in their ivory towers, writing their *Wissenschaft* tomes, immune to the moral tragedy and horror around them. We, members of the Academy, are responsible for our own moral stance and, in a certain way, we are also responsible for the moral education of our students. If teaching is a political act, teaching about the Holocaust is an obligation. We must teach this material.

Given the reservation of non-scholarliness and given the moral and dialogic motivation, what shape should a course on the Holocaust have? At Emory University, we have been experimenting with a syllabus for the past three years which, I think, has proven effective. To begin with, the course is team-taught by a social scientist, Dr. Jack Boozer, who specializes in Christian ethics, and by myself. I strongly recommend this team approach because, if the questions engendered are good, they are offensive, or defensive, and the presence of those who can speak authoritatively for Judaism and Christianity makes the communication easier, though it does not change the truths taught. We have also encouraged a wide range of students to participate, including Christian theology students and lay people from the Jewish community. This sometimes inhibits the undergraduates but it also lends a dimension to the class which it would not otherwise have. We estimate that the class is forty percent non-Jewish. We do not limit enrollment, though we encourage freshmen to wait a year.

As to the syllabus itself, the course is divided into four units. Unit One, usually handled by the social scientist, deals with the background to the Holocaust. We have found Dawidowicz' *The War Against the Jews* Part I, to be most comprehensible for the students. We have also used the film *Triumph of the Will* (shown in two parts for best results and followed by discussion each time) very effectively in making the main point of this unit: that the Holocaust took place in a perfectly normal environment. As one of the students said, "If the Holocaust is about to happen, why are all those people laughing?" It is also necessary to point out that racism, anti-Semitism, volkism, etc., were perfectly normal modes of thinking at the time, even though they are no longer respectable, in most